Kent & East Sussex Railway-based Southern Railway USA 0-6-0T No. 30065 passes Terrace Junction on the Tanfield Railway with a coal train on June 12, 2016. The locomotive was one of a very distinctive and useful class imported into Britain during the Second World War to ease a locomotive shortage, in this case dockyard shunters, as outlined in Chapter 15, and is seen in a post war identity as NCB No. 35, a class member that worked in the Northumberland coalfield in the early Fifties. DAVE HEWITT

RAILWAYS
STILL AT WAR

Designer:
Craig Lamb
design_lamb@btinternet.com

Cover Design:
Michael Baumber

Reprographics:
Paul Fincham and Jonathan Schofield

Publishers:
Steve O'Hara, Tim Hartley

Publishing Director:
Dan Savage

Commercial Director:
Nigel Hole

Marketing Manager:
Charlotte Park
cpark@mortons.co.uk

Distribution Executive:
John Sharratt
tradesales@mortons.co.uk
classicmagazines.co.uk/tradesales

Printed by:
William Gibbons and Sons, Wolverhampton

ISBN:
978-1-911276-02-9

Published by:
Mortons Media Group Ltd,
Media Centre, Morton Way,
Horncastle, Lincolnshire LN9 6JR.
Tel: 01507 529529

FRONT COVER: Southern Railway West Country Pacific No. 21C123 *Blackmoor Vale* (running as *OVS Bulleid*) gets a friendly wave from the local Home Guard as it passes Keynsford Lane during the Bluebell Railway's Southern at War weekend on May 10, 2008. JON BOWERS

MORTONS
MEDIA GROUP LTD

One of the biggest events in the calendar of many of Britain's heritage railways today is their annual Forties or wartime weekends.

We often think of the dark days of the first and second world wars as gloomy and depressing, with everything appearing in varying shades of grey.

Yet every summer, our preserved railways become a riot of living colour, as thousands of re-enactors, some with military vehicles and hardware, reprising roles from soldiers to spivs, major generals to music hall entertainers. Hordes of eager visitors alike descend on them, many retro-dressed for the big occasion.

Everyone seeks to immerse themselves in reminiscences of those hardest of times when our brave island nation stood, for years alone, for freedom and liberty against tyranny of the worst kind.

In 2016, we are also remembering in the centenary of the Battle of the Somme, the pivotal moment in the Great War, when the tide on the Western Front turned in our favour.

Heritage railways are the perfect linear stages on which to re-create dramas and cameo scenes of a yesteryear society in which the train was still, often by necessity, the first choice of transport for most people.

Not only that, but many heritage lines are lucky enough to have locomotives and rolling stock that played key roles in both conflicts, from the trench railways on the Western Front to the War Department Austerity engines turned out in their hundreds to satisfy the ever-hungry needs of a global conflict. Not to mention those we borrowed from the USA through the Lend-Lease agreement.

In this unique publication, we look both at the wartime nostalgia phenomenon as it is played out each year in the heritage sector, and the stories of the locomotives that survived both conflicts and continue to entertain – and educate – us all today. Not to mention the strange and secret places that became time capsules – such as the disused Underground station that Winston Churchill used as a bunker in the Blitz, and the mysterious Second World War railway on a remote island in the Bristol Channel.

Our heritage railway wartime weekends are not just about re-creating part of our proud history while boosting our local tourist economies. These hugely and increasingly popular events are as much, if not more so, about remembering the sacrifices of those servicemen and women who gave their lives to ensure that our country remained safe and had the future we've inherited today.

We must never forget that.

Robin Jones
Editor

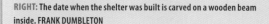

Didcot Railway Centre boats two genuine 1940-built air raid shelters, constructed to protect staff at the town's GWR shed. One used in the centre's Forties events is next to the shop while the other, behind the Great Western Trust Museum and archive, is used as a store and not open to the public. The shelter is made from concrete and protected by being semi-sunk into the ground. The roof is covered with stones, which would have been scattered by a nearby blast, absorbing much of the energy. The air raid shelter on show was restored to its original condition in 2008. FRANK DUMBLETON

RIGHT: The date when the shelter was built is carved on a wooden beam inside. FRANK DUMBLETON

Bagnall Austerity 0-6-0ST No. 2777 of 1945, War Department No. 75254 (175), was sold to the National Coal Board in 1963 as Alloa Area No. 7, and is now back steaming in military guise in preservation on the Bo'ness & Kinneil Railway. SRPS

Take cover! Quorn & Woodhouse station on the Great Central Railway under direct Luftwaffe attack!

IN WAR AND PEACE
WE SERVE

GWR · LMS · LNER · SR

Didcot Railway Centre is a very rare example of a venue where you can authentically use diesel traction in a Forties event. GWR railcar No. 22, which was built in 1940, arrives at Oxford Road station. FRANK DUMBLETON

GREAT WESTERN SOCIETY

Forties fun and frolics on the East Lancashire Railway's Ramsdown (Ramsbottom) station. ELR

Remain in line, please – young evacuees wait for the next train at the North Yorkshire Moors Railway. NYMR

Senior Army officers detain a wartime spiv outside Bodmin General station on the Bodmin & Wenford Railway. JIMMY JAME

We'll meet again: a farewell Forties embrace through an LNER teak coach window on the North Yorkshire Moors Railway. NYMR

The blackout observed in a carriage during a Didcot Railway Centre wartime weekend on September 15, 2013. FRANK DUMBLETON

TRACTION
for the trenches

The First World War was the first major conflict to draw on the fruits of industrial technology, and it was a century ago in 1916 that sprawling networks of temporary narrow gauge railways were laid in the trenches of the Western Front to boost the ruthless efficiency of the slaughter.

If you are searching for an insight into the narrow gauge lines that served the killing fields of northern France during the Great War, the best place to start is the Leighton Buzzard Railway in Bedfordshire.

This 2ft gauge line boasts the biggest collection of Motor-Rail Simplex internal combustion locomotives, which were built in nearby Bedford from 1916 onwards, to keep the supply lines of the battlefields moving, without issuing plumes of smoke to let 'the Hun' know their whereabouts, or emitting sparks that could ignite ammunition.

Secondly, the line dates from 1919, when it was opened as an industrial sand-carrying concern using war surplus locomotives, stock and materials from the trench railways.

Thirdly, it is the base of the Greensand Railway Museum Trust, the prize possession of which is the trench railway's *Flying Scotsman* equivalent – Baldwin Class 10-12-D 4-6-0 No. 778 (works number 44656 of 1917).

Designed in 1915, the 10-12-Ds were built at Philadelphia Locomotive Works during 1916-17 to 1ft 11⅝in gauge for the War Department Light Railways. All 495 built were delivered except for nine that were lost at sea.

Originally intended for the Front Line in Europe, several were allocated to other theatres of war, including the 1917 offensive against the Ottoman Empire in Sinai and Palestine.

After the war, WDLR locomotives and rolling stock were declared Army surplus and sold off.

Class 10-12-Ds went on to work in France, Britain and India. UK narrow gauge railways that used examples included the Welsh Highland Railway, the Glyn Valley Tramway, the Snailbeach District Railways and Ashover Light Railway, but none of these survived the Fifties.

The type, however, is nowadays well represented in the UK heritage sector.

WD No. 794 was brought back from India (where it had worked on a sugar plantation and named *Tiger*) with the aid of a Science Museum PRISM fund grant in 1985 and given to the Imperial War Museum, which planned to restore and run it at its Duxford site.

Baldwin Class 10-12-D 4-6-0 No. 778 on the Somme: the locomotive running on the last-surviving French battlefield line, the Froissy Dompierre Light Railway, on June 3, 2011. CLIFF THOMAS

War Department Light Railways No. 778 departs Page's Park with a train for Stonehenge Works. MERVYN LEAH

Baldwin No. 778 passed its latest steam test at Page's Park on April 12, 2016. CLIFF THOMAS

However, that failed to materialise. In 2004, it was transferred to the Welsh Highland Heritage Railway at Porthmadog, which was eager to receive an example of a type that ran on the original line.

It came as a complete rolling chassis but with the boiler in poor condition. The WHHR is now raising the funds needed to finish its restoration, after which it will run as No. 590, the number carried by the original Welsh Highland example.

Also repatriated at the same time using the grant money was WD No. 778, which, after the First World War ended, was sent to the North West Railway in what is now Pakistan. By the Thirties it was with the Daurala Light Railway in Uttar Pradesh (about 100 miles from Delhi), and it ended its working life at the Upper India Sugar Mills at Khatauli, also in Uttar Pradesh.

While No. 794 was earmarked for the Imperial War Museum, No. 778 was destined for the Amberley Museum in West Sussex.

In 1994, No. 778 was moved from Amberley to the Leighton Buzzard Railway under a long-term agreement. A start was made on dismantling, largely to assess the degree of work required, but work halted.

Early in 2000, a fresh look was taken at how the restoration of the locomotive could be moved forwards. The Greensand Railway Museum Trust was formed in February 2001 and after being registered as a charity, took over ownership of the Baldwin. That year, an appeal was launched in *Heritage Railway* by the Greensand Railway Museum Trust to restore No. 778.

The trust and the railway signed an agreement on November 22, 2002 whereby the locomotive would be based at Leighton Buzzard, a registered museum, and restored under its management.

An application under the Your Heritage scheme for its restoration was made to the Heritage Lottery Fund in February 2003, leading to a £50,000 grant being awarded in May 2004.

On repatriation, the locomotive was totally worn out, but complete and surprisingly original, the principal exceptions being the tanks and bunker, which had been replaced in India. However, the boiler clearly required replacement. The original unit (which may prove to be the original American-built item) has been retained as a static exhibit.

The restoration was project-managed by Adrian Corke, the volunteer chief steam engineer for the Leighton Buzzard Railway for 14 years, until his appointment as full-time engineering manager of the Buckinghamshire Railway Centre. Adrian is now owner and operator of the Evesham Vale Light Railway but continues to oversee engineering aspects of No. 778.

Statfold Barn's two Baldwin 4-6-0Ts repatriated from India in 2013. ROBIN JONES

Under his guidance, No. 778 was restored as close to 'as built' condition as possible while employing the highest-possible mechanical standards for operating in present-day conditions.

A contract to restore the chassis was placed with Alan Keef Ltd of Ross-on-Wye, while Andy Bennett of Bennett's Boilers designed and built a new boiler.

The restoration was fully completed by Alan Keef Ltd and No. 778 moved under its own power for the first time on August 1, 2006. Its first official steam test was passed at Keefs on April 25, 2007 and was delivered back to Leighton Buzzard the following day.There, it steamed the length of the line, and was officially launched during a donors' day on July 14, 2007 when it hauled its first passenger train, a special for people who donated to the restoration project. It entered regular service in August 2007.

In 2011, No. 778 returned to one of the Western Front battlefield lines, fulfilling the

ALCOS CAME TOO

Baldwin 4-6-0Ts were not the only American locomotive type supplied to Britain for the Western Front.

The Cooke works of the American Locomotive Company (ALCO) supplied 100 2-6-2Ts to the War Department Light Railways in 1916.

One example survives in the UK, No. 57166 (WD No. 1265).

After the war, it was used on reconstruction work in north-eastern France for the French government's Ministère des Régions Libérées. Much later, it worked on the Tramway de Pithiviers à Toury.

In 1967, it was bought by Ffestiniog Railway London Area Group member, John Ransom, who had visited that line just before closure. He arranged for the ALCO to be transported to Isleworth in West London where a short length of 2ft gauge track was laid in the grounds of the Osterley Sea Scouts. When John moved from London, he offered the engine to the FR as it needed a new home, and on October 14, 1967 it set off for North Wales. It steamed at Boston Lodge a few days later, entering service in early November.

Named *Mountaineer* on the FR, has been a powerful performer on passenger trains and been rebuilt several times, being converted to oil firing in 1972 and fitted with a new boiler in 1983. It has also visited the Vale of Rheidol Railway.

Mountaineer was withdrawn in February 2006 and is now awaiting its 10-year overhaul, which will include a back conversion to coal firing.

A sister ALCO 2-6-2T is preserved on the Froissy Dompierre Light Railway.

Mountaineer on a Ffestiniog Railway service train in the Seventies. FR

ambitions of the trustees to see it working alongside other survivors of the Great War battlefield supply lines.

APPEVA, the association which has run the Froissy-Cappy-Dompierre line near the town of Péronne right in the Somme battle zone since the early Seventies, agreed to allow it to visit the line.

This line is the last survivor of the vast network of narrow-gauge railways that supplied the battlefields, and Leighton Buzzard is the last survivor of the British lines built with war-surplus materials and equipment in the years following the Armistice.

The French army built the Froissy Dompierre Light Railway in 1915 and after the war assisted with the reconstruction of the villages it served as well as bringing food. New lines were laid including a zig-zag to reach the Santerre Plateau.

In 2009, APPEVA sent ex-military Décauville 0-6-0T No. 1652 of 1916 to take part in the LBR's 90th anniversary celebrations. As well as working alongside No. 778 for the first time, it was filmed for UK national television, appearing several months later in the series John Sergeant on the Tourist Trail.

Agreement was reached for No. 778 to take part in the French line's June 2-5, 2011 gala event celebrating 40 years of preservation of the Froissy-Cappy-Dompierre line, and its 10 years of twinning with Leighton Buzzard.

After visiting several UK heritage railways, No. 778 was taken out of service in September 2015 on expiry of its boiler certificate and taken to Alan Keef Ltd for overhaul, the boiler being retubed by Locomotive Maintenance Services in Loughborough, but thanks to donations to a nationwide appeal, underwent a fast-tracked boiler overhaul and returned to service in early 2016, being booked to make a second visit to the Somme line in May that year.

On March 21, 2013, two more Class 10-12-Ds arrived in the UK, at Graham Lee's private Statfold Barn Railway near Tamworth, which has a track record second to none in acquiring scrap narrow gauge engines from the Far East and rebuilding them to as-new condition.

The pair were No. 44657 of 1916 (WD No. 779 and the next in line after No. 778) and No. 45190 of 1917 (WD No. 618).

Both engines were returned from the war to the UK and were overhauled by Bagnall – giving them something of a UK pedigree – before being sold to India. No. 779 was sold to the Indian Army Reserve, then to TATA Ltd and then to the Ryam sugar factories in Bihar state.

No. 1058 was sold to the Indian Army Reserve and then to the North Western Railway as its No. 45 and later also passed to the sugar factories.

One other Class 10-12-D (No. 45215 of 1917) is preserved on the Dreamworld Railway in Coomera, Queensland, Australia, and is under overhaul.

Built in 1929 to a First World War design is Motor Rail 20hp petrol-mechanical four-wheeler No.21 *Festoon* (works No. 4570), which may well be a rebuild of a wartime machine. Initially used on contracting work, it was sold to the George Garside quarry company in 1931, and hauled sand trains at Leighton Buzzard. It survived the arrival of newer diesels, by being converted to a self-propelled fitters' workbench, and is the oldest locomotive original to the heritage line. To mark the Simplex centenary in 2016, it went on display at the John Higgins Museum in Bedford, from mid-April. GEOFF TRIBE

THE SIMPLEX STORY

While Baldwin produced vast quantities of locomotives for the trench railways, the Motor Rail & Tramcar Co Ltd of Bedford was equally prolific. However, this was a case of modern technology for a modern war being fought with technology on an industrial scale.

Baldwin built steam, but Motor Rail provided petrol-and diesel-engined locomotives, still very much a rarity on railways of the time, yet which have come to represent the definitive engine type associated with the temporary tracks of the Western Front.

Formed in 1911, in January 1916, the company answered a War Department tender for military supply railways. The specification was for 1ft 11⅝ in gauge locomotive, with no more than one ton of axleload per axle, capable of hauling up to 15 tons at 5mph.

May 2016 marks the centenary of the start of production of around 900 such internal combustion locomotives by the firm for the War Department Light Railways and the Ministry of Munitions.

The company designed a new locomotive, based around a square-set but with outer longitudinal 'bent rail' frame, mounted on two axles. The 2JO petrol engine manufactured by WH Dorman & Co of Stafford was centre-set longitudinally in the frame. This arrangement resultantly required the operator to sit above the engine facing to one side of the design, to enable mounting of the engine and Dixon-Abbott patent gearbox, which drove the unsprung axles through a chain drive. The water-cooling radiator was mounted to the front of the locomotive, and a large fly wheel gave relatively smooth operation.

A second but armoured version was made to a specification defined by the Ministry of Munitions. This used an upgraded Dorman 4JO 40hp engine and two-speed gearbox, coming in three versions: firstly, open: armoured end plates plus height-adjustable canopy on pillars; secondly, protected: as open, plus armoured side doors and visors, and thirdly, armoured: completely enclosed with armour-plated roof, and end slits for the driver to look through.

There were 11 basic models, some petrol some diesel powered, some 20hp, others 40hp, and variants of each. I have always thought of them as railway Daleks; in the science fiction series Dr Who, the Daleks were designed as protective moveable casings housing a living creature with guns attached, and this is exactly what these were. The Daleks too were born out

A rare working survivor of the "protected" (lightly armoured) 40hp petrol locomotives built for the War Department Light Railways, after the war, several of this type were used to haul sand trains at Leighton Buzzard, but all were scrapped by the end of the Fifties. LR3098, which was built in Bedford in 1918, worked at Knostrop sewage works, Leeds, and is owned by the National Railway Museum, York, where it returned in the summer of 2016. MERVYN LEAH

of necessity, the product of an endless war between two races.

The trade name Simplex was used from the early days, and in 1972 the company was renamed Simplex Mechanical Handling Ltd.

After the war, as with other war surplus stock, vast quantities of Simplexes came on to the market cheaply. Being more economical and easier to operate and maintain than steam locomotives they found ready buyers in industry.

Including Leighton Buzzard, at least 20 narrow gauge lines or museums have at least one representative of the type.

At Leighton Buzzard, the original 20hp Simplex type was used in the line's construction, and subsequently employed on quarry branches, while the larger 40hp version replaced steam on its 'main line' in 1921. It is believed that it was the first railway in the UK to be operated entirely by internal-combustion power, nearly a century ago.

Diesel engines replaced petrol from the Thirties onwards. In 1987, locomotive manufacture ceased, and the business line was sold to Alan Keef, which continues to provide spares and has built several locomotives to Motor Rail design.

Alan himself launched his own book about Motor Rail at a Simplex centenary held at Leighton Buzzard during May 28-30 and June 1 and 4-5. On Sunday, May 29, a record bid for the largest number of Simplexes ever to pull a train was attempted on the last train of the day, the 4.25pm departure from Stonehenge Works.

STANDARD GAUGE WESTERN FRONT SURVIVORS

During the Great War the Railway Operating Division of the Royal Engineers requisitioned about 600 standard gauge locomotives of a wide assortment of types from 13 British railway companies, the first arriving in France in late 1916.

Only two of those locomotives survive today.

The first is North British 0-6-0 No. 673, which was built at Cowlairs Works in 1891.

In 1917, No. 673 was sent to the Western Front to work supply trains and was named after a famous military leader of the day, Lt Gen Sir Frederick Stanley Maude.

Maude returned in 1919 and hauled freight trains until it was withdrawn from Bathgate shed in July 1966. The Scottish Railway Preservation Society saved it from the scrapman and now it is part of its collection at the Bo'ness & Kinneil Railway, the sole-surviving example of a 'typical' Scottish freight engine.

The second is GWR 43XX class 2-6-0 No. 5322, which, built in Swindon in 1917, was sent new to the Western Front in response to a call from the Army that summer for UK railways to supply a further 160 locomotives to help with transporting supplies from the Channel ports to the front line.

Frank Potter, general manager of the GWR, insisted that in return for the supply of 2-6-0s, which were desperately needed for use at home, the government should supply sufficient materials to enable five new engines of the class to be built each month.

A serving officer with the ROD, CER Sherrington, recalled an encounter with No. 5322 in France in 1918, in an article about it for the Great Western Echo in 1973:

"That night nearing the level crossing at Pont des Briques, where one turned off for the mess, an eastbound train was rapidly overtaking me. A glance at my watch led me to hope that it was Ravitaillement Calais-Ligne No. 21 running on time from Calais (Riviere Neuve) to St Omer, Hazebrouck and one or more railheads. There was no mistaking the type of locomotive – by the beat of its exhaust – a GWR Mogul, thus confirming that it was, almost certainly, one of the 53s doing such splendid work on

Simplex No. LR2182 is the only known survivor, in original mechanical condition, of the fully armoured version of the same LR3098. Built in 1917, LR2182 went to a brickworks near Barrow, where it lost the upper part of its armour plating. In the Sixties it was bought privately for preservation from a scrapyard, and found its way to the Museum of Army Transport in Beverley, East Yorkshire, with the missing armour replaced with plywood.

It was donated by the Museum of Army Transport to the Leighton Buzzard Railway. In preparation for the LBR's 90th anniversary celebrations in 2009, new wooden replacements for the armour were made and installed, and other transit damage repaired. This allowed it to take its rightful place in the superb displays of First World War military motive power.

The Greensand Railway Museum Trust, owner and operator of Baldwin No. 778, is appealing for the funds required to also return this unique machine to full working order, complete with full armour.

The original Dorman petrol engine, which has not been fired up for more than 50 years, has now been removed for inspection and reconstruction, as has the transmission, with its early example of a Dixon-Abbott gearbox. Both have been found to be in predictably poor condition, and applications have been made for grants towards restoration ahead of its centenary, when it is hoped it will run again for the first time in six decades. The engine and transmission have been removed for attention.

The trust has been awarded £11,500 under the Arts Council for England PRISM Fund, plus £500 from the Museum Development Bedfordshire Small Grants Scheme, for the project, but more is needed. Anyone who wishes to support the appeal is invited to visit www.buzzrail.co.uk and download a form.
GEOFF TRIBE

North British 0-6-0 No. 673 *Maude* in pre-Grouping livery at Bo'ness. RON HANN*

GWR 2-6-0 No. 5322 in Railway Operating Division khaki livery at Didcot Railway Centre on September 4, 2008. FRANK DUMBLETON

RIGHT: The bracket supporting the rear of the roof of the cab of No. 5322 has been crudely cut away to allow clearance for the butt of a .303 rifle placed in it. FRANK DUMBLETON

those supply trains.

"It overtook me at the Pont des Briques crossing, with its metal rolling gates, and it was easy to see its number in large white letters on the tender – ROD 5322. Behind it were the customary 44 or so wagons, the supplies for two divisions. The gross load was some 770 tons: the wagons were not vacuum fitted, but, of course, had the French screw couplings.

"The Great Western Moguls were admirable locomotives for this work: their predecessors on it, the Beyer Peacock 4-6-4 tanks, which were built for the Netherlands but never got there, were splendid machines but had inadequate brake power, being designed for suburban passenger trains. The LNWR Class 27 0-8-0s, though fine pullers, had small diameter wheels for this work, and were more suited to heavier, slower, trains."

No. 533 was released from war duties at Chester in 1919, and was finally withdrawn from Pontypool shed depot in April 1964.

It ended up in Dai Woodham's Barry scrapyard, and in 1969 was bought by a member of the Great Western Society and at first moved to Caerphilly for restoration.

In 1973, it moved to Didcot Railway Centre and ran there for two years before it was stopped. It then passed into society ownership, and returned to traffic in November 2008.

For several years, it carried its ROD khaki livery.

In November 2011 the locomotive was disguised as a Russian locomotive and starred in a film version of Anna Karenina, and it May the following year, it was outshopped in BR black livery.

No. 5322 was withdrawn in summer 2014 with boiler problems.

Sister GWR 43XX 2-6-0 No. 5319 in France during the First World War. FRANK DUMBLETON COLLECTION

Simplex No. 264 on display inside the Welsh Highland Heritage Railway's museum at Gelert's Farm in Porthmadog. WHHR

First World War Simplex *Mary Ann* in action at Porthmadog Harbour station on October 8, 2010, during a Ffestiniog Railway vintage weekend. PETER TRIMMING*

SIMPLEXES IN SNOWDONIA

Steam remains by far and above the defining image of railway preservation. Therefore, it may come as a surprise to many that the first train on one of the world's finest heritage narrow gauge railways was hauled by an internal combustion locomotive.

On September 21, 1954, a 1917-built Simplex numbered 596, later named *Mary Ann*, became the first locomotive to haul a passenger train over the first section of the revived Ffestiniog Railway following the saving of the line by businessman and future *Flying Scotsman* owner Alan Pegler.

Built as a petrol tractor for service in the First World War, it was among the many sold off after the war as Army surplus. The pre-preservation Ffestiniog Railway bought it in July 1923 from the Kent Construction & Engineering Company of Ashford in Kent for £350 for shunting on the wharves of Portmadoc and Minffordd.

Its identity is not definitively known. It carries the builder's plate No. 507 of 1917, but that locomotive is recorded as having been rebuilt by Motor Rail for the Leighton Buzzard Railway. It was fitted with the bodywork from No. 596, a Protected Simplex, although the frames and running gear were from an open model.

As the price of petrol was deemed to be too high, Col Holman F Stephens, the light railway magnate who at the time controlled both the FR and sister Welsh Highland Railway, ordered it to be converted to kerosene burning, reducing running costs to 60% of those of a steam locomotive.

Stephens wanted to use it on winter passenger services on the WHR, but the Board of Trade refused permission. While it was good enough for shunting and work on the level, it could haul only two bogie carriages on the gradients of the main line and could not be used in passenger service without fitting a vacuum brake.

In 1971, it was named *Mary Ann* after general manager Allan Garraway's mother Connie's name for a maid-of-all-work.

In recent times, an overhaul included the reinstallation of a petrol engine, a new fuel tank, new bonnet and a larger radiator. It no longer carries a name.

Meanwhile, the separate Welsh Highland Heritage Railway in Porthmadog has two beautifully restored internal combustion locomotives that both saw service in the First World War.

The first is Motor Rail Simplex 20hp petrol tractor No. 264 of 1916. Supplied to the War Department, it later worked at Porton Down (the nuclear, biological and chemical research establishment), before being bought for preservation. Its original petrol engine had been replaced with a similar one at some time before it came to Wales.

It arrived on the WHHR in 1997, restoration to full working order began in 1998, and the engine became operational once more in July 2009. By October that year, the locomotive was able to move under its own power again, managing to haul eight tons on test, with a surprising turn of speed. A similar 'bow-framed' locomotive, albeit a 40hp version, was used in 1941 on the Welsh Highland Railway demolition train.

The second is Baguley 15hp 0-4-0 No. 760 of 1918 .... pictured on page 31 (in Apedale Trenches chapter). It was previously based on the Abbey Light Railway near Leeds and is unique in being the only working example of its type anywhere in the world. Very lightweight, and owing to a lack of air brakes and the wrong sort of coupling, it cannot be run on passenger trains, but on test it has hauled in excess of 10 tons.

Built to operate on the Western Front trenches, it is designed to run on lightweight 9lb track, and is narrow to fit down trenches with a short wheelbase to negotiate sharp corners. It is believed that locomotives such as these had a life expectancy of about three weeks on the front line. They were built to work alongside the better-known Simplexes.

However, the design proved to have flaws as although the loco was narrow, the driver stands up quite high, and the clutch (which originally was operated by the handbrake wheel) proved difficult to operate. These problems led to the locos being used away from the frontline, in tank depots and for logging, where there were

also tight corners. There exists evidence that one of them was used in a sleeper yard of the LNER.

To commemorate the centenaries of both trench railways in 2016 and that of No. 264, the WHHR has built a new interactive diorama in its museum at Gelert's Farm.

It allows visitors to appreciate the locomotives and the service they provided to the military during the war. Once inside the museum building, visitors are invited to imagine they are in Bazentin-le-Petit; a devastated village near the Somme battlefield in the late autumn of 1916.

The idea is that the building represents the 'office' of the Royal Engineers 7th Field Company, which has built (and been left to run) a 60cm (2ft gauge) tramway system supplying part of the Front north of the Somme. Research revealed detailed diaries, which included commentary from a man called John Glubb, who was 19 at the time and an acting captain. (He went on to become General Glubb 'Pasha', a key influence on the Royal Jordanian Army after the Second World War.)

One of their bases was in a quarry near the ruined village of Bazentin-le-Petit. They used Simplexes like 246 and might have tried out (and found unsatisfactory) a Baguley.

Inside the office, where battery-powered flickering candles illuminate the dark interior, a flat-screen TV shows a video describing the role of the trench tramways and their early development, which ultimately led to the formation of the War Department Light Railway Department.

Sandbags, corrugated iron and lots of camouflaged paint have been used and even a 'trench' has been created along the mural wall behind the locos. The end result is very effective and initial feedback from visitors is very positive.

The creation of the exhibit has been a co-operative effort on the part of many of the volunteers at the Welsh Highland Heritage Railway. New volunteers are always welcome at the railway: for more details visit www.facebook.com/WHHRly

FROM FLANDERS FIELDS TO POTATO FIELDS

Another classic example of a job lot of Army surplus trench railway equipment being snapped up was Lincolnshire's Nocton Estates, which bought enough rolling stock and track materials to create a 23-mile network around its farms which produce potatoes for Smiths Crisps.

Some of the ex-WD stock including 1920-built Simplex Nocton, was in 1960, bought by the Lincolnshire Coast Light Railway Company for use on its new 2ft gauge line at Humberston, near Cleethorpes. Incidentally, the LCLR at the time made history by becoming the first heritage railway in the UK to be built on a green field site.

One of the Class D bogie open wagons was converted into an open passenger coach and ran in this form until 1985. Class Ds were designed to have the equivalent capacity as a standard 10-ton wagon and could be adapted to carry stretcher cases.

In 1981, the Lincolnshire Coast Light Railway Historic Vehicle Trust was formed to care for a Class P wagon, two Class D bogie wagons and the line's bogie ambulance van. The trust moved the wagons to the now-closed Museum of Army Transport at Beverley, East Yorkshire and was able to restore them there.

The LCLR closed in 1985, but in 1992 relocated down the coast to Skegness Water Leisure Park and recommenced train

The restored Class D wagon No. 2572 at Skegness on April 2016. DAVID ENEFER

services in 2009. In 2004, the trust's First World War vehicles were moved there.

In 2015 Class D bogie wagon No. 2572, funded to the tune of £47,000 by the Big Lottery through ITV's People's Millions, was restored to its original condition of 1916 with the addition of access for disabled passengers. When in service, passengers can now ride in an open bogie wagon just as the soldiers of the British Army did from 1916 to 1919.

The frames of No. 2572 (before restoration) showing shrapnel damage from First World War activities. The frames have had new strengthening members added but still retain this damage on view. DAVID ENEFER

REACH THE WESTERN FRONT BY BUS!

The B-type, developed by the London General Omnibus Company was the first successful mass-produced motor bus. Designed and built in London, they quickly ousted horse buses and trams from the capital's streets, and by 1913 there were 2500 B-type buses in service, each carrying 340,000 passengers per year along 600 miles of busy roads in and around London.

With the support of the Heritage Lottery Fund and the Friends of London Transport Museum Friends, the award-winning Covent Garden museum's B2737 was restored to operational condition. It was launched in June 2014 in its original red and cream livery, and attended 14 public events over that summer.

In September that year, the bus was converted into a military troop carrier, like so many of its sister vehicles had been in 1914, to commemorate the role of London's transport workers during the First World War.

As a military vehicle it attended a number of events, including a 10-day commemorative tour of Western Front locations in Belgium and France.

The 'Battlebus' as it is known, is seen crossing Westminster Bridge. JOHN STILES/LTM

The locomotive of the First World War

During the First World War, the need for a standard locomotive to use in British military operations at home and overseas by the Railway Operating Division of the Royal Engineers was identified. GCR chairman, Sir Sam Fay, a member of the Railway Executive Committee, persuaded the government to choose his company's John G Robinson 8K 2-8-0 for the purpose.

The first Great Central Railway 8K heavy freight 2-8-0, No. 966, emerged from the company's workshops at Gorton in Manchester in September 1911. Basically, it was a superheated version of the earlier 8A class 0-8-0, with a pony truck added to support the greater front-end weight and give a steadier ride. The type was introduced to handle increased levels of traffic as a result of the company's vast new docks complex at Immingham near Grimsby and by June 1914 there were 126 in traffic. During the First World War there were experiments with oil-burning 8Ks with larger bogie tenders.

The outbreak of the war led to the Royal Engineers forming its Railway Operating Division (ROD), which began operations in continental Europe in February 1916. The Army originally intended to use French and Belgian locomotives, but both of these countries deliberately kept their locomotives away from the Front.

Accordingly British locomotives were 'called up', and at first comprised a motley collection from the nation's many railways

BELOW: Rebuilt O4/8 No. 6311, which was built in 1919 to a government order, heads a train of empty mineral wagons at Worksop sidings on June 17, 1957. BEN BROOKSBANK*

BR black-liveried GCR O4 No. 63601 approaches Kinchley Lane with a mixed freight during the winter gala on January 27, 2007. ROBIN JONES

in those days before the Grouping of 1923.

The powers that be quickly decided that standardisation of locomotives was needed, and the ROD chose the GCR's 8K design, which was proven to be robust and straightforward, steamed well and was outstandingly reliable. GCR Chief Mechanical Engineer John G Robinson held the opinion that the 8K was his best design.

Orders for 325 locomotives were placed in February 1917, and they were followed by orders for 196 more in 1918 in order to keep British industry going during the postwar run-down in military manufacturing.

The ROD 8Ks differed from the GCR originals only in minor details, such as the fitting of Westinghouse air brakes and the use of steel for the boiler tubes and inner firebox.

The First World War had led to an increase in the cost of coal and deterioration in its quality. Robinson became interested in the use of coal dust, which also offered the promise of total combustion, and four O4s were used for pulverised fuel experiments between 1917-24.

WAR SURPLUS

After the war, the redundant 8Ks were loaned or sold to many of Britain's railways. As the price of war surplus 8Ks plummeted, many ended up with the LNWR, its successor the LMS, the GWR and some were even sold as far afield as China and Australia.

A further 19 locomotives were built by the GCR in 1918-21 to a modified design with a larger boiler, and these became Class 8M. In 1922 the GCR rebuilt two Class 8Ms to 8Ks.

The LMS 8Ks were all scrapped or sold by the Thirties, and half of the GWR fleet was gone by 1930, while some survived well into the Fifties.

Under the LNER, the 8Ks became O4s, and the 8Ms became O5s, although all of the latter were converted to O4s. The LNER bought 273 former ROD locomotives in 1923-27, bringing its O4 fleet to 421.

It was on the LNER that they became a mainstay of freight traffic and also the most numerous of LNER heavy goods locomotives.

Indeed, the O4s become one of the most successful British steam locomotive designs of the 20th century.

A total of 92 of these were requisitioned by the War Department in 1941, for use in the Middle East, where a supply route through Persia to Russia had been opened, and none of them returned to Britain.

They were written off the LNER's books in December 1943. In 1940, the GWR borrowed 30 O4s from the LNER, returning them between 1941-43.

Fifty-eight O4s were rebuilt by Edward Thompson into O1s in 1944-49, and 329 O4s were inherited by British Rail at Nationalisation in 1948.

Five were sold to the government in 1952 for use in Egypt.

Withdrawals of O4s began in December 1958 and ended with the last examples bowing out of service in the Doncaster area in April 1966.

GCR O4/1 No. 63664 at Langwith Junction engine shed on August 7, 1960. RUTHAS*

Contributors to its nationwide restoration appeal were invited to a special viewing of O4 No. 63601 back in steam on the Great Central Railway on a murky January night in 2000. The National Collection engine is seen hauling the line's Windcutter rake of mineral wagons through Swithland. The engine was unveiled to the public at a gala weekend immediately afterwards. ROBIN JONES

FOUR SURVIVORS

Four O4s have survived into preservation, one in Britain and three in Australia.

As an example of one of the most successful steam locomotive designs ever and one of the final three O4s surviving with a Belpaire boiler, No.63601 was chosen for preservation in 1960 as part of the National Collection.

One of the first of the class to head heavy freight trains to and from the enormous new port of Immingham, No.102 emerged from Gorton Works in January 1912. It was renumbered 5102 in June 1925, 3509 in April 1946, 3601 in February 1947 and finally 63601 in September 1949.

Its first allocation was to Gorton on March 14, 1912, and this was followed by transfers to Sheffield, Mexborough, Barnsley, Doncaster, Frodingham near Scunthorpe and Immingham.

In addition to the heavy freight traffic to and from the docks, the locomotive was involved in the development of the

steelworks at Frodingham.

Having undergone very few modifications from its original condition, it was withdrawn from service at Frodingham in June 1963.

With storage space for preserved engines then being in short supply, No. 63601 first went to Doncaster Works, then Stratford and Brighton. It then moved to Leicester to be housed in a proposed Leicester Museum of Technology at Abbey Meadows Technology Museum.

That project having failed to take off, in 1976 No. 63601 returned to GCR metals in the form of the engine shed at the long-closed Dinting Railway Centre.

Locomotive department staff there decided it was restorable, and No. 63601 was sent to Longsight depot to have its axlebox repaired.

In 1977, Dinting staff said that a completely new tender would be needed because the one fitted to the locomotive was vacuum and not steam braked.

The restoration carried out at Dinting was purely cosmetic. When the centre closed, No. 63601 was sent to the National Railway Museum in York.

By that time, there were many voices calling for the locomotive to be restored because of its historical importance. The Main Line Steam Trust, which had established the modern-day Great Central Railway, was instrumental in bringing it to Loughborough in June 1996.

A national appeal was launched to raise more than £70,000 – the cost of restoration to full working order –with the trust contributing £25,000.

An exhaustive restoration programme entered its final stages on June 18, 1999, when the retubed boiler passed its steam test before being lowered back into the frames four days later.

Unpainted, it was displayed in light steam during the August 7-8 gala that year.

Finally, on January 24, 2000, it moved under its own steam for the first time in 36 years.

Four days later, it was coupled to the Windcutter rake of 16-ton mineral wagons and ran through Swithland Sidings for the benefit of contributors to the national appeal. Its full public debut came the next day at the start of the winter gala weekend.

During the replacement of hundreds of copper boiler side stays in 2001, a new smokebox together with an LNER pattern chimney were fitted.

No. 63061 has visited other heritage lines including Keighley and Worth Valley and the Churnet Valley railways as well as Barrow Hill. It appeared at the National Railway Museum's Railfest 2012 event in June that year.

Its final run on the GCR came on June 24, 2012, its last passenger train departing from Loughborough Central at 5.30pm. By that time it had been based on the heritage-era GCR for 16 years, five more than it had run in traffic for the original company.

After its withdrawal, talks with the National Railway Museum about a second overhaul for another decade on the GCR began.

GCR O4 No. 63601 passes BR Standard 2MT 2-6-0 No. 78019 as it enters Rothley with the Windcutter rake on October 9, 2006 during the annual autumn steam gala. ROBIN JONES

RIGHT: Robinson O4 No. 63601 storms towards Quorn & Woodhouse station during the Great Central Railway's 'Golden Oldies' gala on May 31, 2010. ROBIN JONES

In July 2009, No. 63601 visited the heritage-era GCR's northern sister line, the Great Central Railway (Nottingham), for the July steam gala at Ruddington. In 2016, work began on building a bridge over the Midland Main Line at Loughborough to link both heritage railways, and create an 18-mile inter-city heritage route between the outskirts of Nottingham and Leicester. Coupled with progress at Ruddington on restoring several original GCR wooden-bodied carriages, there are hopes that one day an overhauled No. 63601 might haul a genuine all-GCR train over it. BRIAN SHARPE

The boiler of Great Central Railway-built ROD No. 23 on its frame at Richmond Vale Railway Museum in NSW, Australia, on January 21. The 2-8-0 has been cosmetically restored. GRAHAM BLACK

WILL THEY EVER COME HOME AGAIN?

The three O4s that survive in Australia are the last survivors of 13 RODs bought from the War Department during the Twenties by the mining firm of J&A Brown in New South Wales. J&A Brown operated the 18-mile Richmond Vale Railway from a connection with the New South Wales Government Railways at Hexham, to the collieries at Pelaw Main and Richmond Main, the largest coal producer in New South Wales.

Two of them, Nos. 20 and 24 (ROD Nos. 1984 and 2003) are owned by the Dorrigo Steam Railway and Museum Limited in New South Wales.

To date, none of them has been restored to working order in preservation and while their service makes them part and parcel of Australian transport heritage, over the years there have been inquiries about repatriating one or more to the UK, maybe for restoration in the livery of one of the companies other than the GCR or LNER that used them.

In 2016, *Heritage Railway* magazine revealed that several UK heritage lines had turned down the offer of No. 23.

Built at in Gorton in February 1919, it was one of only six built for ROD by the GCR itself. Most of the others having been supplied by either North British or Robert Stephenson & Co.

Numbered 2004 by ROD, it was sent to France as the last member of the class to be shipped across the Channel. It returned six months later and was loaned to the GCR, until being placed in storage in November 1921 and offered for sale by the War Department.

As J&A Brown No. 23, on February 15, 1973 when working a train of loaded hopper wagons at Hexham, it had become the last ROD locomotive to operate on the main line anywhere in the world. It was withdrawn on June 8, 1973, when, with 627,184 miles on the clock, nearly seven years after BR took the last O4 out of traffic.

In 1978 it was taken to a nearby mining museum, but in 1986 returned to its long-time home, moving to Richmond Vale Railway Museum, which is located on the site of the former Richmond Main Colliery. No. 23 spent 28 years at the museum as unsuccessful attempts were made to raise funds for a restoration and return to steam.

By the end of 2014, the museum could afford a cosmetic restoration. However, Graham Black, the museum's mechanical branch manager had hoped for many years to see No. 23 fully restored and returned to steam, and accordingly had approached many UK heritage lines in vain.

The deal on the table would be for a heritage railway to pay the shipping costs for it to return to Britain, overhaul it, run it in traffic until all costs had been recovered, and then return it to Australia in working order.

It is said that the last O4s operating in China were retired in 1990.

Storm clouds are gathering as O4 No. 63601 hauls a passenger service during the Great Central Railway's 2004 wartime weekend. ROBIN JONES

Lining up alongside GER J17 0-6-0 No. 65567 at Barrow Hill Engine Shed's LNER II gala on April 3, 2009, are GCR O4 No. 63601 and Improved Director No. 506 Butler-Henderson. ROBIN JONES

The pair of ROD O4s stored at the Dorrigo Railway Museum in New South Wales. Might one or both ever return to the UK? MIKE RUSSELL*

In the loop: GCR Class 8K No. 23 at work at Six Mile Loop on the J&A Brown colliery line in NSW, Australia, in 1967. The 2-8-0, which is being cosmetically restored, worked on the line for nearly 50 years and in 1973 became the last ROD locomotive to operate on the main line anywhere in the world. British heritage railways have turned down the opportunity to bring the loco back to the UK for overhaul and a return to service. RICHMOND VALE RAILWAY MUSEUM COLLECTION

Great War
ambulance trains

The First World War not only saw railways play an unprecedented role in the waging of trench warfare, but also the emergence of the ambulance train to carry wounded servicemen back from the front lines.

A Harry Payne oilette from early in the First World War, when French goods wagons were used to transport the wounded. It shows the Royal Army Medical Corps at work.

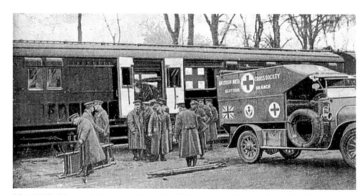

A Scottish Red Cross ambulance at work near the firing line on the Western Front, bringing patients to the ambulance train for transmission to a base hospital. The vehicle was donated to the British Army Medical Services by the Scottish branch of the British Red Cross Society. The proceeds from the sale of such hand-coloured postcards went to the Red Cross.

THE LSWR coach, which has been used to re-create a First World War ambulance train. ROBIN JONES

RIGHT: The museum's Adrian Ashby applies the red cross emblem, during preparations for the Ambulance Trains exhibition. NRM

LEFT: This re-created ambulance train will form the centrepiece of the National Railway Museum's new exhibition. It opens on July 9, 2016 to mark the centenary of the busiest day of the Battle of the Somme. ROBIN JONES

30-325 OO Scale Train Pack

www.bachmann.co.uk

FIRST WORLD WAR
AMBULANCE TRAIN № 40
— SPECIAL COMMEMORATIVE EDITION —

Contains a GWR City Class 3711 'City Of Birmingham', Three Midland Railway Ambulance Coaches and a pack of WWI Medical Staff and Soldier Figures.

Modelmaker Bachmann issued this special OO gauge GWR ambulance train pack to mark the centenary of the outbreak of the First World War.

A landmark exhibition highlighting the history and crucial role that ambulance trains played in the First World War and beyond has been set up by the National Railway Museum.

The event was timed to open on July 9, 2016, the centenary of the busiest day of the Battle of the Somme.

The centrepiece of the Ambulance Trains exhibition, already on display in the Great Hall, is a carriage once owned by the Ministry of Defence.

Built in 1907 for the LSWR, the carriage is of the type that would have been converted for use in an ambulance train.

It has been carefully transformed both inside and out to enable visitors to step on board and move through a ward, a pharmacy and a nurses' mess room.

Digital projection, sound and historic images, alongside re-created interior fittings, will bring to life the intense atmosphere of these confined trains.

Years of painstaking, detailed research

Beds made and ready inside an ambulance train in April 1918. NRM

An ambulance train at Huddersfield station, 1916. NRM

by experts at the York-based museum has uncovered the forgotten stories of the people who travelled on British ambulance trains, from the injured soldiers transported to hospital, to the medical staff who offered the best care they could in cramped, difficult and stressful conditions.

Ambulance trains were not a First World War innovation. The first hospital train was built in the 1850s during the Crimean War, as a response to public concern in Britain over inadequate provisions for the British army and the well-being of their soldiers during the siege of the Russian port of Sevastopol. To address the worsening situation, the Grand Crimean Central Railway was built initially by a partnership of English railway contractors led by Samuel Morton Peto in 1855, to supply ammunition and provisions to Allied soldiers. Within three weeks of the arrival

of the fleet carrying materials and men, and in seven weeks, seven miles of track had been completed.

Although this railway's primary function was the supply of armaments and equipment, its train was also used for the transport of the wounded. The first such instance of this occurred on April 2, 1855, when a train was used to carry the sick and injured from the plateau down to the dock at Balaclava.

The railway was a major factor leading to the success of the siege.

Similar trains were subsequently used during the Franco-Austrian War, the American Civil War, the Franco-Prussian War and the Anglo-Zulu War, but on board medical facilities were sparse, although nurses accompanied the wounded and the carriages were painted with red crosses to highlight their humanitarian role and prevent enemy attack.

However, it was during the First World War that trains began to be used as mobile medical facilities along the Western Front.

The ambulance trains were organised by the Royal Army Medical Corps with on board surgical wards and essential medical supplies, and were used to evacuate more than 100,000 British casualties from the battlefield at Flanders in just one month of 1914 alone.

The first British ambulance trains on the Western Front consisted of a few empty French goods wagons with straw laid on the floor.

At the end of August 1914, the RAMC was given three locomotives and a further number of goods wagons and a few carriages. They were converted and divided into three 'trains'. Each consisted of wards, surgical dressing rooms and dispensaries and were designated British Ambulance Trains 1, 2 and 3.

The RAMC continued converting French rolling stock up to train number 11, and in November 1914, the first purpose-built medical train was sent out from the UK and designated No. 12. No train was given the number 13 and near the end of the war, number 43 arrived in France.

Several of the trains were built with voluntary contributions. For example, No. 12 was Lord Michelham's, No. 15 was Princess Christian's and the United Kingdom Flour Millers paid for No. 16.

These trains connected with hospital ships at Channel ports to repatriate wounded British soldiers back to England. Many were referred to as 'Great White Hospital Trains', as the carriages were often painted white, or red and white.

Millions of men were brought to Britain from the Front via these tightly packed trains, which included fully equipped wards, pharmacies and kitchens. The trains were manned by resident medical officers, orderlies and nurses and could be up to a third of a mile long.

Phillip Gibbs of the Daily Chronicle

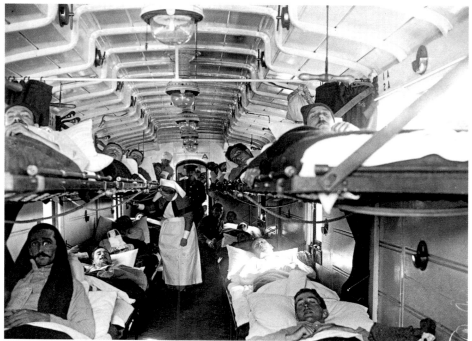

Patients on board a First World War ambulance train. WILLIS FAMILY COLLECTION

An ambulance train car being loaded at Tilbury Docks in 1915, on its way to the Front. NRM

The infectious diseases ward in a LNWR ambulance train, about 1917. NRM

A nurse boards a French Red Cross train bearing sick and wounded soldiers to Paris.

The railway yard at Balaclava, where the world's first hospital train operated, during the Crimean War. ROGER FENTON

Nurses line up alongside their ambulance train in 1916. NRM

observed a long ambulance train pulled up near the village of Chocques and rapidly fill up with men suffering all kinds of wounds.

He reported that the first to board were thousands of "lightly wounded", he said, who "crowded the carriages, leaned out of the windows with their bandaged heads and arms, shouting at friends they saw in the other crowds. The spirit of victory, and of lucky escape, uplifted these lads... And now they were going home to bonny Scotland, with a wound that would take some time to heal."

Next to board were those who came on stretchers, "from which no laughter came". Gibbs reported that one young Cockney, "was so smashed about the face that only his eyes were uncovered between the bandages, and they were glazed with the first film of death".

Another young soldier, "had his jaw blown clean away. A splendid boy of the Black Watch, was but a living trunk. A group of blinded men was led to the train

Servicemen standing beside a Midland Railway ambulance train on August 27, 1914. NRM

One of the narrow gauge ambulance cars in First World War use.

by wounded comrades, 'groping', very quiet, thinking of a life of darkness ahead of them..."

The museum's interpretation developer Jane Sparkes said: "Until now historians have overlooked the crucial role that ambulance trains played in the First World War, but careful research by our curators and archivists has gradually uncovered this neglected piece of history.

"The mass casualties of modern mechanised conflict called for evacuation of the injured on a scale never seen before, and this simply could not have happened without these trains."

"For the first time, our exhibition will bring together photographs, technical drawings, letters and diaries to bring to life the huge range of human experiences carried on board these trains.

"The Ambulance Trains exhibition has been designed to explore stories of the wounded soldiers who travelled with their harrowing memories of warfare, and the medical staff who worked tirelessly in claustrophobic conditions to provide comfort and care.

"It also looks at the railway workers who built the carefully designed trains at incredible speed to keep up with demand, and the wider public who saw the grim reality of the overseas war when these trains pulled into British stations."

Associate museum archivist Alison Kay said: "Ambulance Trains is the culmination of years of work, and it is incredibly gratifying to give these trains and their passengers the 21st-century prominence they deserve through this new exhibition.

"The museum's research team has examined hundreds of historic documents and photographs describing life aboard the trains, and all accounts of life on board have a real emotional impact."

The exhibition has been supported by both the Heritage Lottery Fund, which contributed £98,000 towards it, and Yorventure, via Yorwaste through the Landfill Communities fund.

The exhibition programme includes a series of free talks by curators, experts and descendants of ambulance train staff, with

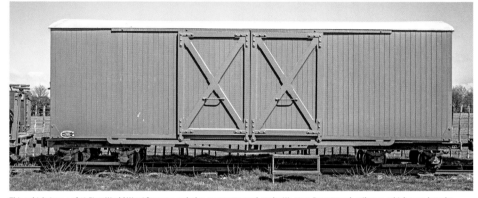

This vehicle is one of 12 First World War 2ft gauge ambulance wagons used on the Western Front trench railways, which were bought secondhand by the Nocton Estates Company in Lincolnshire, for use on its extensive system serving its potato fields, each box van having a six-ton capacity. It was later acquired by the Lincolnshire Coast Light Railway and is part of its museum collection at its current Skegness Water Park base at Ingoldmells. DAVID ENEFER

a special trail for families to explore the displays together.

Fiona Spiers, head of the Heritage Lottery Fund in Yorkshire and the Humber said: "The impact of the First World War touched every corner of the UK. Thanks to National Lottery players an important part of our First World War history has been brought to light; the restored ambulance train will be on show alongside significant

stories and research showing the essential role that they played in the war effort."

Hospital trains were used on a large scale during the Second World War by all the major combatants and also to a smaller extent during the Korean War.

By that time, however, mobile motor transport and aerial evacuation replaced the train as the primary form of mobile medical provision on the battlefield.

A Great Western Railway ambulance train, as depicted in a hand-coloured postcard. Such trains were run by all the major British railway companies to take wounded soldiers back to their home towns.

Western Front west of Stoke on Trent!

Life, often brief, in the muddy disease-ridden trenches of the Western Front was a horror that servicemen who were lucky enough to return from preferred to forget. A trench system complete with sandbagged trenches, lookout posts, a supporting 2ft gauge railway and a fleet of historically appropriate locomotives and stock has been built in the Potteries to remind modern generations of the experience.

All quiet for the moment on Staffordshire's version of the Western Front. ROBIN JONES

The Greensand Museum Trust's 1917-built Baldwin Class 10-12-D 4-6-0 No. 778 at Apedale station during the 2014 Tracks to the Trenches event. MRT

A new dimension has been added to Britain's heritage railway portfolio to mark the centenary of the outbreak of the First World War.

During the glorious sunshine of September 13-14, 2014, the Moseley Railway Trust's 2ft gauge Apedale Valley Light Railway near Newcastle-under-Lyme held the first of its Tracks to the Trenches wartime events.

The showpiece event brought together what was believed to be the largest number of surviving First World War narrow gauge locomotives in the history of preservation.

In the months leading up to the event, volunteers constructed a replica of a Western Front trench railway system, complete with operational tracks, something that is unique in Britain today.

A conservative early estimate indicated that more than 3000 visitors attended. For the first time, both the trust's collection of First World War Motor-rail Simplex petrol tractors and others visiting for the event could be seen operating in the genuine trench environment for which they were designed by the Bedford-based manufacturer. Indeed the gala was the first time that all four types of Motor Rail internal combustion locomotives used on the War Department railways were reunited.

Steam locomotives from both sides of the conflict were also in action, with the Greensand Museum Trust's First World War US-built Baldwin 4-6-0T No. 778 from Leighton Buzzard and home-based Kerr Stuart Joffre 0-6-0T No. 3014, built in 1916 for use on the Western Front, sharing duties with one from the other side, 1918-built Henschel 'Brigadelok' 0-8-0T No. 1091 (15968) of 1918.

Nearly 2500 'Brigadeloks' were built for the German military light railways or Heeresfeldbahn, and like the Baldwin tanks, found ready buyers in private industry after the Armistice was signed.

Another guest was the Phyllis Rampton

Squaddies ask for directions from the driver of the Moseley Railway Trust's Kerr Stuart Joffre 0-6-0T No. 3014 of 1916, which served on the trench railways in France. MRT

Baldwin 4-6-0T No. 778, 'Brigadelok' 0-8-0T No. 1091 and Kerr Stuart Joffre 0-6-0T No. 3014 during a night-time re-creation on September 9. ROBERT FALCONER

Foden Type W military compound steam road lorry works No. 7768 and Hudswell Clarke 0-4-0WT No. 1238 of 1916 meet. ROBERT FALCONER

Western Front veterans Baldwin No. 778 and Kerr Stuart Joffre No. 3014 rub shoulders at Apedale station. ROBIN JONES

Trust's Kerr Stuart Wren 0-4-0ST No. 3114, which was built for the War Department in 1916, but did not get any closer to the Western Front than Eastburn Aerodrome near Driffield.

They ran alongside Hudswell Clarke G class 0-4-0WT No. 1238 of 1916, which had been restored to as-new condition, despite being left to rust in a Ghanaian swamp for 48 years before being rescued and eventually repatriated.

While this particular G never saw military service, it is representative of a type built in large numbers at the company's Foundry Works in Leeds for the trench railways and other theatres of the Great War.

It was one of a pair exported from the Harrington Dock, Liverpool via the *SS Prahsa* to the Ashanti Goldfield Corporation in Ghana. No. 128 worked near Akrofuom, a locality in the Obuasi district. In 1952 it fell into a river during a storm, killing its driver.

It was recovered in 1995, and placed on display outside a museum at Anglogold Ashanti's mine complex at Obuasi. Following negotiations, its owners allowed it to return to its country of origin, which it did aboard the *MSC Samantha*, sailing from Tema in Ghana to Felixstowe, arriving on May 5, 2008.

It was delivered to Apedale nine days

later, and then restoration began.

It was joined at Tracks to the Trenches by the Statfold Barn Railway's Hudswell Clarke 0-6-0WT No. 1643 of 1930 No. GP39 formerly known as *Bronwllyd*, and built to the same G class design.

The site's re-created trench closely mirrored those of 100 years ago, being positioned behind three hedges, which within months, may have been replaced by bomb craters. Indeed, one popular exhibit was that of a Simplex, which had toppled into such a crater.

Re-enactors in First World War British uniforms manned the trench, drove the locomotives and populated a tented Army

Apedale Valley Light Railway volunteers busy laying the new field railway in time for the Tracks to the Trenches event in 2014. MRT

Hudswell Clarke 0-6-0WT No. 1643 of 1930 No. GP39 on the field railway system. ROBIN JONES

Petrol tractors scurry about their business on the Apedale field railway. ROBIN JONES

Protected Motor-Rail tractor No. 1381 of 1918 No. LR3101 visiting the 2014 Tracks to the Trenches gala from the Amberley Museum & Heritage Centre. Built for the Western Front, it did not get any further to the action than Purfleet wharf in Essex.

camp that had mushroomed behind.

Not only that, but the cavalry in the form of the 16 Lancers pitched in too!

Following success of the widely acclaimed event, the biggest in the Apedale Valley Light Railway's comparatively short history, the trust was announced as the joint winner of the 2014 Heritage Railway Association Annual Award (Small Groups), along with the Downpatrick & County Down Railway.

The Moseley Railway Trust was honoured for amassing a unique collection of industrial locomotives as well as the re-creation of the trench railway with appropriate traction and rolling stock as an invaluable educational resource.

The trust also won the John Coiley Locomotive Award for its funding and restoration of No. 1238.

The trust subsequently launched a new First World War trench railway driver experience.

Participants are transported back in time nearly 100 years to Northern France during 1917, where they sign-up with the 6th Light Railway Operating Company.

After instruction, participants are given a series of challenges, which they must meet by driving both steam and diesel locomotives around the railway network at Apedale, including the replica trench.

Participants were given the option of having their midday meal as hard tack biscuits and a mess can full of tea in the trench.

Kerr Stuart Joffre No. 3014 paused alongside protected Simplex No. 3090. MRT

The sole-surviving (out of 34 built) 40hp armoured Motor Rail Simplex, War Department Light Railways 'Tin Turtle' No. 2182 (No. 461 of 1917) still with its original petrol engine. Now in the care of the Greensand Railway Museum Trust based at the Leighton Buzzard Railway. After the First World War, it worked at the Furness Brick & Tile Co Ltd at Askam-in-Furness, near Barrow, and was later preserved at the former Gloddfa Ganol museum in North Wales and then at the now-closed Museum of Army Transport at Beverley in Yorkshire. ROBIN JONES

An armoured car on the Apedale battlefield. ROBIN JONES

This unfortunate Motor-Rail petrol tractor had toppled over into a bomb crater, now liberally protected with barbed wire, a trademark feature of the trenches. MRT

A tender military encampment well back from the front line and the range of bullets and missiles. ROBIN JONES

RIGHT: The cavalry charge in! ROBIN JONES

BELOW: The 16 Lancers give a military horsemanship demonstration at the award-winning first Tracks to the Trenches event at Apedale in 2014. MRT

A long way from the London Underground station, this section of a re-created First World War trench at Apedale was given the nickname Piccadilly Circus. ROBIN JONES

Many of the troops who entered the trenches did so in the knowledge that they would probably never leave them alive. ROBIN JONES

The sleeping quarters inside the trench. All it needs is dirt, grime, squalor and rats to add authenticity. ROBIN JONES

Welsh Highland Heritage Railway-based Baguley 15hp four-wheeler 0-4-0 No. 760 of 1918 was one of a type originally intended to operate close to the Front Line, but, they suffered from glowing exhausts when working hard, which made them ideal targets for enemy snipers. ROBIN JONES

Riding behind a miniature protected Simplex 'Tin Turtle' during the 2014 Tracks to the Trenches event. ROBIN JONES

FROM THE CLASSROOM TO THE FRONT LINE

Apedale Valley Light Railway operator the Moseley Railway Trust has its origins in a railway society based at Moseley Hall Grammar School in Cheadle near Stockport. As a school project, its then very youthful members started to lay a circular 2ft gauge track (the Moseley Tramway) around the perimeter of a playing field.

At first, the line used materials obtained from a local brickworks, including a brick car, which formed the basis of the initial horse-drawn vehicle.

As time progressed, diesel, petrol and battery-electric motive power arrived and the collection started to grow with several public open days taking place.

At the end of 1996, however, owing to redevelopment and adaptation of the Margaret Danyers College, as the site had become known, into its expanding role as a tertiary college, the railway was given notice to vacate. This enforced move prompted the trust, as it had by then become, to develop a museum and railway on a new site completely from scratch.

Restored War Department Light Railways flat wagon No. LR3571 loaded with supplies including missiles. ROBIN JONES

From its humble beginnings as a schoolboy society, the trust had amassed the biggest collection of industrial narrow gauge locomotives and rolling stock in the country, including many items with a military background.

In 2007, the newly established 454-acre Apedale Community Country Park at Chesterton near Newcastle-under-Lyme, which was being developed on the site of an opencast coal-mining area, was identified as an ideal place in which to relocate.

An earlier scheme to create a 2ft 6in gauge Apedale Valley Railway on part of

the former Midlands Coal & Iron Company system in what later became the country park had stalled. However, the trust saw its potential as a 2ft gauge heritage line and set about developing a railway, workshops and museum complex in conjunction with the existing Apedale Heritage Centre. The aim was not just to preserve and showcase industrial heritage but to act as a catalyst in the regeneration of the Apedale/Chesterton area.

During 2007, many items from the former Cadeby Rectory Railway arriving at the Apedale site swelled the collection.

Trust's Kerr Stuart Wren 0-4-0ST No. 3114 was built for service on the Western Front, but never got there... until 2014. It is pictured alongside a First World War tank on the Apedale battlefield. MRT

A SECOND BATTLE IN STAFFORDSHIRE!

Responding to public clamour for another First World War event, a second Tracks to the Trenches event was held at Apedale from May 13-15, 2016, marking the centenary of the Battle of the Somme, considered to be the turning point in the conflict.

The battle could not have been fought without the logistical support provided by the narrow gauge railways used by both sides to move supplies and troops up the front lines and into areas where it was too dangerous for full-size trains to operate.

At the event – which was again sponsored by railway magazine publisher Mortons of Horncastle – from its base at the West Lancashire Light Railway was Kerr Stuart No. 2405, built in 1915.

This 0-6-0T is the oldest survivor of the type known as the Joffre and duly carries that name. The type is named after Marshal Joffre – known as Papa – one of the key leaders of the French military effort, especially in the early part of the First World War.

This visit reunited this locomotive with the Joffre-class resident No. 3014.

Making a return visit was Baldwin No. 778 (works number 44656 of 1917) from the Leighton Buzzard Light Railway, having just completed a major boiler overhaul. It was one of the stars of the 2014 event.

Ahead of the gala, the trust's trench railway network was given a £10,000 Heritage Lottery Fund boost.

The money was earmarked for the trust's interpretation of the role of the horse in delivering supplies to the front lines.

During the 1914-1918 conflict, both sides used horses not only for direct combat (cavalry regiments) but also as a means of moving the huge weights of supplies that a fighting army needs to sustain it.

Light railways were laid as a means of increasing the amount a horse could haul,

and also to spread the weight of wagons in the mud of Flanders fields and elsewhere.

Frequently, supplies would be hauled by

steam-or petrol-powered locomotives to a point near the front lines, and then horses were used for the last mile to the

Squaddies pausing for a breather with Kerr Stuart Joffre No. 3014 between rounds of shellfire. MRT

Hudswell Clarke G class 0-4-0WT No. 1238 of 1916 which, unlike its sisters, never made it to the First World War battlefields and so avoided having to run the gauntlet of bombs and shrapnel, but instead rotted in a swamp for 48 years. You would never have thought it looking at its today. The Heritage Railway Association's John Coiley Award for 2014 was made to the Moseley Railway Trust for its restoration. ROBIN JONES

Hunslet No. 1215 of 1917 in First World War service. WOLT

AN ABSENT COMRADE

Sadly, however, the War Office Locomotive Trust's Hunslet 4-6-0T No. 1215 of 1916 was not able to attend the May 2016 Tracks to the Trenches event to celebrate its centenary, as had originally been hoped for.

Several delays to its restoration had been encountered – as is inevitable when restoring 100-year-old machines. The owners and the trust both decided that the best course of action was to ensure that the highest-quality restoration was completed, rather than rushing to meet the May deadline.

Now unique in the UK, it was one of 145 ordered for the War Department Light Railways, and duly left its builders, the Leeds works, on December 8, 1916.

It was later seen operating at Boisleux-au-Mont in the Pas-de-Calais with troops from the American Expeditionary Force.

After the war, Hunslet bought back the locomotive, rebuilt it, and sold it to the Engineering Supply Company of Brisbane,

Australia. That company sold it on to Gibson & Howes Ltd at Bingera Sugar Mill, Bundaberg, for use on the vast network of sugar cane railways in Queensland.

Named *Hunslet*, it was reboilered in 1942, and worked until 1956 when it was sold to the Invicta Sugar Mill.

Invicta's own Hunslet, No. 1226, needed a new boiler, and so the cab and tanks were fitted to No. 1215, which then worked for a further eight years.

After storage, No. 1215 was presented to the Rowes Bay Children's Home in 1967. It stayed there until 1994, when an enthusiast bought it for restoration.

The War Office Locomotive Society then bought it and repatriated it to the UK, arriving on September 16, 2005. It was displayed at the Locomotion museum at Shildon and later visited the Leighton Buzzard Railway and Hollycombe Steam collection before its arrival at Apedale on July 13, 2008.

Kerr Stuart Joffre No. 2405 in service at Apedale. MRT

front – the so-called trench tramways.

Using the grant, the trust will replicate these operations and demonstrate them to visitors.

The grant will also allow permanent improvements to the facilities and exhibits at Apedale. Volunteers are building an extension to the existing demonstration railway and an interpretative panel, both will further enhance the Industrial Railway Trail, which was initially funded by the Lottery Fund in 2014.

A trench tramway wagon will also be constructed. These vehicles were hauled by horses on the very lightly built railways that spanned the vital last yards to reach the troops fighting at the front.

Vanessa Harbar, head of Heritage Lottery Fund West Midlands, said: "The impact of the First World War was far reaching, touching and shaped every corner of the UK and beyond. Our small grants programme is enabling even more communities to explore the continuing legacy of this conflict and help people to broaden their understanding of how it has shaped our modern world."

Repatriated Hunslet No. 1215 undergoing restoration at a private site in England. WOLT

Heroine of HUMANITY

"Patriotism is not enough".

Norfolk heroine of humanity, Edith Cavell.

Those were some of the final words of nurse Edith Cavell, who was shot by the Germans on October 12, 1915 for helping wounded British and French soldiers escape from occupied Belgium.

While the German action was legal under international law, it provoked worldwide outrage, and immortalised the 49-year-old for her courage, and above all, compassion.

Born in the Norfolk village of Swardeston, Edith was the daughter of a rector and worked as a governess in Belgium, before training as a nurse in London. After working in hospitals in Shoreditch, King's Cross and Manchester she accepted a position in Brussels as matron in Belgium's first training hospital and school for nurses. Her pioneering work led her to be considered the founder of modern nursing education in that country.

Edith returned to Norfolk to visit her mother in 1914, but after war broke out and hearing of the threat to Belgium from the advancing German troops, she returned to Brussels.

By August 20, Brussels was occupied by the Germans. The nursing school became a Red Cross hospital – treating casualties from both sides – as well as continuing to treat civilians.

That September Edith was asked to help two wounded British soldiers trapped behind German lines following the Battle of Mons. They were treated in her hospital before she arranged to have them smuggled out of Belgium into The Netherlands, which was neutral.

Over the next 11 months, she aided around 200 British, French and Belgian soldiers, sheltering them in the hospital and arranging for guides to take them to the border.

The Germans had been suspicious of her activities long before arresting her on August 5, 1915, as she had been betrayed by Gaston Quien, who was later convicted by a French court as a collaborator.

After being placed in solitary confinement in St Gilles Prison in Brussels,

Restored South Eastern & Chatham Railway PMV No. 132 carried the coffins of two of Britain's greatest First World War heroes and also that of the Unknown Soldier. KESR

LEFT: The KESR's London Chatham & Dover Railway third-class carriage No. 3062, with the Cavell van and LBSCR A1X 'Terrier' 0-6-0T No. 32678, at Northiam station on November 11, 2011. No. 3062 had just been restored to as-built condition following 65 years of use as a bungalow after its withdrawal from traffic in 1921, and this was its first day back in service. HUGH NIGHTINGALE

Photographed on the Diamond Jubilee of Queen Elizabeth II on June 5, 2012, the replica coffin of The Unknown Warrior inside the Cavell van is adorned with 60 fresh poppies. HUGH NIGHTINGALE*

she was tried at a court martial on October 7, along with 34 other people linked to her escape network.

After admitting her role in the escapes, she was found guilty of treason and sentenced to death. Despite worldwide appeals for clemency, including some from local German authorities, Edith was shot by a firing squad on October 12, 1915.

German civil governor Baron von der Lancken is known to have stated that Cavell should be pardoned because of her complete honesty and because she had helped save so many lives, German as well as Allied. However, General von Sauberzweig, the military governor of Brussels, ordered that "in the interests of the state" the implementation of the death penalty against Baucq and Cavell should be immediate, denying higher authorities an opportunity to consider clemency.

I always balk at references to her death as an execution, which as such was legal under international law. Most of her fellow defendants at the court martial were not sentenced to death, and the German authorities had the power to show clemency. To me, it was state-sponsored murder.

At the time, the fate of a pioneering nurse who had not only helped Allied troops but also treated wounded enemy soldiers caused huge outrage not only in Britain but also in many then-neutral countries, including the United States. Far from sending out a 'zero tolerance' message of behalf of the Germans, Edith became a figurehead for a just cause, and her fate became invoked in Army recruitment posters.

On instructions from the Spanish minister, Belgian women immediately buried her body next to Saint Gilles Prison.

HOMECOMING WITH HONOURS

In May 1919, her body was exhumed and taken back to Britain for a memorial service at Westminster Abbey and was transferred to Norwich, to be laid to rest at Life's Green on the east side of the cathedral. King George V had to grant an exception to an Order in Council of 1854, which prevented any burials in the grounds of the cathedral, to allow the reburial.

Edith's body was transported with full military honours from Dover to London, by South Eastern & Chatham Railway, using the prototype of a new series of box van, the Diagram 960 PMV (Parcels and Miscellaneous Van) – known in the USA as boxcars – which was ceremonially fitted out with a catafalque and hung with drapes.

No. 132 was built in 1919 at Ashford Works as the first of more than 1600 vans of the type built by the SECR and the Southern Railway up to 1951. The subsequent production vehicles became dubbed Cavell vans by railwaymen.

Two months later, on July 15, the same van carried the body of another national hero who had also been shot in cold blood by the Germans. Great Eastern Railway employee Cpt Charles Fryatt was transported from Dover to Charing Cross with full military honours.

THE RAILWAY CAPTAIN AND THE SHOW TRIAL

In 1892, Fryatt joined the GER as a seaman on *SS Ipswich*, following in the footsteps of his father, who had been the First Officer on *SS Cambridge*. Charles Fryatt rose through the ranks, and his first command was *SS Colchester*.

On March 3, 1915, Fryatt's command, *SS Wrexham*, a Great Central Railway vessel was attacked by a German U-boat. His ship was chased for 40 nautical miles and reached 16 knots when 14 knots would normally have been the upper limit. *SS Wrexham* arrived at Rotterdam with burned funnels.

In gratitude for his actions, the GCR presented Fryatt with a gold watch inscribed "Presented to Captain C. A. Fryatt by the chairman and Directors of the G.E Railway Company as a mark of their appreciation of his courage and skilful seamanship on March 2nd, 1915. Later the same month, the captain was in charge of Colchester when it was unsuccessfully attacked by a U-boat."

On March 28, 1915, when captaining

Father-of-seven Cpt Charles Fryatt (December 2, 1872- July 27, 1916), was the Great Eastern Railway steamship captain who was shot by the Germans for defending his ship against an attacking U-boat.

A portrait of nurse Edith Cavell as she sits in a Brussels garden with her two dogs before the outbreak of war. Jack, the dog on the right, was rescued after her death. IMPERIAL WAR MUSEUM

A propaganda stamp issued shortly after Edith Cavell's death. Her fate at the hands of the German army boosted recruitment drives both in Britain and eventually the USA after it joined the war late in the day. In terms of public relations, her death was a massive own goal for Germany. That begs the question – what would have been the result had the Germans showed compassion and commuted her death sentence? Would more people outside their borders been prepared to listen to their cause?

The basis for the charge was based purely the inscriptions on his watches.

On July 27, Fryatt was tried at a court martial in Bruges Town Hall; a show trial.

Not a member of the British armed forces, and acting only in defence of his ship, with no resulting casualties to the Germans, he was found guilty of being a 'free shooter' and sentenced to death – a sentence confirmed by the Kaiser.

At 7pm the same day, the captain was shot by a firing squad and buried in a nearby cemetery used by the Germans for burying Belgian traitors.

MORE INTERNATIONAL OUTRAGE

On July 31, 1916, Prime Minister Herbert Asquith issued a statement in the House of Commons: "I deeply regret to say that it appears to be true that Captain Fryatt has been murdered by the Germans. His Majesty's Government have heard with the utmost indignation of this atrocious crime against the laws of nations and the usages of war. Coming as it does contemporaneously with the lawless cruelty towards the population of Lille and other occupied districts of France, it shows that the German High Command, under the stress of military defeat, have renewed their policy of terrorism. It is impossible of course to conjecture to what atrocities they may proceed."

In a letter to Captain Fryatt's widow, the king called his death an "outrage". Afterwards, soldiers chalked Captain Fryatt's name on artillery shells.

GER chairman Lord Claud Hamilton MP, denounced the killing of Fryatt as "sheer, brutal murder". The New York Times said Fryatt's death was, "deliberate murder" while the New York Herald called it, "the crowning German atrocity".

The Dutch branch of the League of Neutral States presented the GER with a memorial tablet, which was erected at Liverpool Street station. It was unveiled on July 27, 1917, exactly a year after Fryatt's death.

Hundreds of merchant seamen and

A hand-coloured postcard depicting Great Central Railway steamship *SS Wrexham* leaving Grimsby Docks. It was while captaining *SS Wrexham* that Charles Fryatt outran an enemy ship to reach port safely. A gold watch presented to him in acknowledgement of his bravery led to a later decision by the Germans to shoot him after a court martial.

the *SS Brussels*, he was ordered to stop by U-boat 33 near the Maas lightvessel. The U-boat had surfaced to torpedo his ship, so Fryatt ordered full steam ahead and proceeded to try to ram U-33, which was forced to crash dive.

This time round, Fryatt was awarded a gold watch by the Admiralty, inscribed, "Presented by the Lords Commissioners of the Admiralty to Chas. Algernon Fryatt Master of the S.S. Brussel in recognition of the example set by that vessel when attacked by a German submarine on March 28th, 1915." He was also praised in the House of Commons.

However, on June 25, 1916, after *SS Brussels* left Hoek van Holland bound for Harwich, the ship was surrounded by five German destroyers and captured.

Fryatt, 43, and his crew were sent to the civilian internment camp at Ruhleben near Berlin. On July 16, 1916, it was reported in the Dutch newspaper De Telegraaf that Fryatt had been charged with sinking a German submarine – despite the fact that the Germans knew full well that U-33 had not been sunk, and indeed, was on active service at the time the charge was laid.

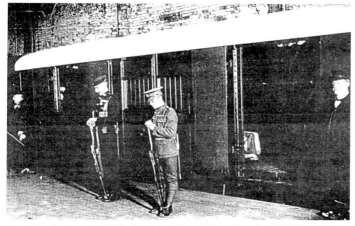

Two soldiers stand guard outside the Cavell van at Dover station on November 10, 1920, before it conveyed the coffin of the Unknown Soldier to London. The union flag-draped coffin can be seen inside. IMPERIAL WAR MUSEUM

A Belgian postcard depicting the scuttling of *SS Brussels* at Zeebrugge by the Germans in October 1918 when they withdrew from the port. The ship was raised by the Belgian government and presented to the Admiralty in 1920. She was repaired and later renamed *Lady Brussels*. She was employed as an Irish Sea ferry, serving until scrapped in 1929.

representatives of the government attended Fryatt's funeral in St Paul's Cathedral. His body was taken back to his home county and buried at All Saints' Church, Upper Dovercourt, Essex.

No. 132 was in the spotlight again on November 10, 1920, when it conveyed the coffin containing the body of the Unknown Soldier from Dover to London's Victoria station. A plaque on the station commemorates the arrival of this train.

The unidentified body had been selected at random from a French battlefield to represent the many thousands of soldiers who had died in the unimaginable conditions of the trenches but had no marked grave.

The following day, the coffin was placed on a gun carriage and with ceremony fit for a field marshal was taken to the unveiling of the Cenotaph by the king.

The coffin was placed a wreath of red roses and bay leaves and followed the gun carriage to Westminster Abbey for the burial.

The tombstone, bearing an inscription to a "British warrior unknown by name or rank," is the only one in the abbey on which it is forbidden to walk.

THE VAN SAVED AS A MEMORIAL

Afterwards, No. 132 was used on regular main line services, until 1946 when it was relegated to being used as a stores vehicle working between Lancing carriage works and Brighton.

It was later used as staff and tool van at Guildford cable depot before being placed in store.

Preservation came when it was purchased by the Tenterden Rolling Stock Group and delivered to the Kent & East Sussex Railway in 1992.

Two years later it was transferred to the nearby Rother Valley Railway, but returned to the KESR in 2004, five years later, the KESR launched an appeal for its restoration.

It became the subject of a fast-track restoration costing £35,000, of which

SS Brussels, a passenger ferry steamer built in 1902 for the Great Eastern Railway, pictured during the First World War.

In memoriam: from left, Norman Brice (KESR chairman), Coun John Holland (Mayor of Ashford), Coun Alan Sugden (Mayor of Tenterden), Elizabeth Carter and Jane Reeves (both Royal London Hospital League of Nurses), and a Royal British Legion standard bearer, at the launch of the Cavell van restoration appeal at the Kent & East Sussex Railway's Tenterden Town station on December 3, 2009. LEWIS J BROCKWAY

The Wells & Walsingham Light Railway's second articulated Garratt, *Norfolk Heroine*, named in honour of nurse Edith Cavell. TIMOTHY TITUS*

LEFT: The plaque fixed to the side of van No. 132. MICHAEL ROOTS*

£27,000 was met by the Heritage Lottery Fund, and was rededicated on November 10, 2010.

The restoration included the re-creation of the interior of No. 132 as it was 90 years before, complete with altar, drapes, and a replica of the Unknown Warrior's coffin, built by KESR volunteers and placed on a catafalque covered by the union flag.

On November 5, 1920 one David John Williams, of Brunswick Ironworks in Caernarfon was summoned to London to make iron bands and eight handles for the oak coffin.

Ninety years later, Meurig Williams, David's grandson and now the owner of the ironworks his grandfather founded, was commissioned by the KESR to re-create the handles and bands for the replica coffin to be placed within the restored van.

Further features are four information panels on Edith Cavell, Cpt Fryatt, the Unknown Warrior, and the histories of Ashford's railway heritage, the van itself and British Pathé Film Archive newsreels of the three funeral processions as well as scenes from the trenches.

During the ceremony KESR chaplain Rev John Emmott rededicated the van – originally painted brown with blue wheels and an authentic white roof, so coloured to enable the many who lined the route to pay their respects 90 years ago to identify the vehicle. In attendance were Admiral Lord Boyce, Lord Warden of the Cinque Ports, representatives of Royal London Hospital's League of Nurses – the hospital where Edith Cavell trained – standard bearers from the Royal British Legion, and students and staff from Tenterden's Homewood School who researched and designed three of the Cavell van's information panels.

The four-wheeled van was returned to running order so that it may be used in special trains and as a national educational asset for schools. However, it serves arguably a far greater purpose – to remind us of how the best of humanity has suffered at the hands of its very worst.

Preserved at the Colonel Stephens Museum in Tenterden, it is often displayed at the KESR's Bodiam station.

HONOURING THE NORFOLK HEROINE IN HER HOME COUNTY

In October 1915, No. 132 was taken by low-loader to Edith's home county of Norfolk to mark the centenary of her death.

The van was displayed on a section of track inside The Forum in Norwich during mid-October.

On October 12, the Wells & Walsingham Light Railway placed a wreath on its Garratt 2-6-0+0-6-2 *Norfolk Heroine*, which was built two years earlier and was named for her.

Running four miles between Wells-next-the-Sea and Walsingham – a major pilgrimage centre since medieval times – on the trackbed of the GER Wells branch, the WWLR is the world's longest 10¼in gauge line.

It is also the world's smallest public railway, an accolade long held by the 15in-gauge Romney Hythe & Dymchurch Railway and briefly by the 12¼in gauge Réseau Guerlédan in France in 1978-79.

It was built by Arctic Convoy veteran Lt Cdr Roy Francis who came from Forncett St Mary near Norwich and served on *HMS Edinburgh* during the Second World War.

On its final voyage in 1942, the ship was loaded with more than four tons of gold bullion as payment from Russia to the UK and the USA for tanks, aircraft and other military hardware desperately needed to halt the Nazi advance.

The ship was repeatedly attacked from German ships and U-boats on May 2, 1942 and sank with the loss of 58 crew lives.

After a long battle with bureaucracy, Roy finally collected his Ushakov medal, offered by the Russian government to

Floral tributes to Edith Cavell were laid on her grave at Norwich Cathedral during the display of van No. 132 between October 5-17, 2015. NICHOLAS WHEATLEY/COLONEL STEPHENS MUSEUM

SECR PMV No. 132 on display outside Norwich Cathedral in October 2015. NICHOLAS WHEATLEY/COLONEL STEPHENS MUSEUM

British seamen who served on the Arctic convoys.

Roy also served on board the *HMS Manchester*. He left the Navy in 1958 and launched a boat-building company on the Norfolk Broads called Rowan Craft.

A railway enthusiast, in the Sixties and Seventies, he took miniature steam trains to fetes and fairs. In 1972, Norfolk engineer, David King, built a 10¼in gauge 0-4-2, *Edmund Hannay*, for Roy, and four years later he opened the mile-long 10¼in gauge Wells Harbour Railway along the flood bank from Wells Harbour to Pinewoods in Wells-next-the-Sea.

Roy sold the line in order to develop a longer 10¼in gauge line on the northern end of the vacant GER trackbed to Wells, the southern part of which is now the Mid-Norfolk Railway.

Pilgrim, an 0-6-0T, also built by David King, launched the line's public service on April 6, 1982. In 1986, a new superheated 2-6-2+2-6-2 Garratt locomotive, *Norfolk*

Hero, named after Admiral Lord Nelson, was introduced to traffic. Predating the operation of articulated reimported South African Railways' Garratts on the Welsh Highland Railway, at the time it was the only example of the type operating in Britain.

A redundant GER signalbox was relocated from Swainsthorpe, a station on the main London to Norwich line, which closed in 1954, to Wells and was converted into a shop and tearoom.

Roy died in his sleep on January 27, 2015 at the age of 92, leaving a wife, Marie, son Rowan, daughter Susie, three grandchildren and two great grandchildren.

One of Peterborough's hospitals is named after Edith Cavell and one of numerous monuments to her in Britain and Europe is located inside the city's cathedral.

Cpt Fryatt is remembered in the naming of the Captain Fryatt Memorial Hospital in Harwich.

The memorial to Cpt Charles Fryatt at Liverpool Street station. STZHANG*

A guard of honour alongside PMV No. 132 was staged when it was displayed outside Norwich Cathedral on Monday, October 12, the centenary of Edith Cavell's death at the hands of the German army. NICHOLAS WHEATLEY/COLONEL STEPHENS MUSEUM

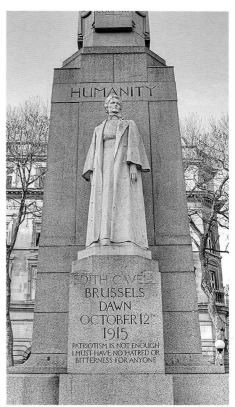

The Edith Cavell Memorial in St Martin's Place, London. PRIORYMAN

Beamish remembers WW1 a century on

In 2016, a year in which venues across Britain organised events to mark the centenary of the First World War and in particular the Battle of the Somme, crowds flocked to Beamish Museum for its April 7-10 Great War Steam Fair, with military and industrial railways of those dark days at the forefront.

No way through – unless you have the protection of an armoured Simplex! BEAMISH

Set in 300 acres of countryside, Beamish Museum in County Durham provides a stunning evocation of North East transport of times past.

The 1825 Pockerley waggonway, which features working replica locomotives from the dawn of railways, has been laid on a decidedly greenfield site, while there is a short North Eastern Railway passenger line based on relocated Rowley station, designed to reflect life in 1913.

Another railway re-creates a typical colliery scene, with pithead wagons and sidings, based around a colliery village. There is also an expanding 2ft gauge line.

More recently a wooden-railed early horse-drawn waggonway has been laid

TOP: On loan to Beamish from the Bristol Harbour Railway is Avonside 0-6-0ST No. 1765 of 1917 *Portbury*. It was ordered after the government took over Britain's docks and harbour during the First World War, and currently carries the Inland Waterways & Docks wartime grey livery in which it served on the Port of Bristol and Avonmouth lines. BEAMISH

Comrades in arms: Western Front locomotive types represented by Hudswell Clarke G class No. 1238 of 1916 and 20hp Simplexes No. LR4978. BEAMISH

Britain's newest steam locomotive, Stephen Lewin replica *Samson*, on display in light steam. BEAMISH

to complete a fuller picture.

The centrepiece of the museum is the town, where original Victorian buildings have been taken down and reassembled to create street scenes. You can visit the Annfield Plain Co-Operative store, a terrace of professionals' houses from Gateshead, the Sun Inn from Bishop Auckland, a branch office of the Sunderland Daily Echo, a bandstand from Gateshead and even a Masonic temple from Sunderland.

A street tramway forms a circuit of the site, linking the town and the railway venues by restored tramcars from the early 20th century.

Beamish took on its first two staff members in 1970 under the auspice of founder director Frank Atkinson. The first tram entered service in 1973 and in July 1975, the Queen Mother visited the museum a month before it welcomed its 500,000th visitor.

Over nearly five decades, Beamish has amassed a sizeable collection of railway artefacts from closed or modernised lines.

Like many heritage railways, it has also developed into a superb stage in which to re-create scenes from the past.

The Great War Steam Fair attracted more than 18,300 visitors as it re-created the roads and railways of the Home Front during the First World War, including military vehicles, around 20 road steam vehicles, lorries, cars and traction engines.

Military groups set up a Gordon Highlanders camp and Royal Army Medical Corps in the pit village and Durham Pals in the town.

The Moseley Railway Trust, whose Apedale Valley Light Railway near Newcastle-under-Lyme has been the venue for the acclaimed Tracks to the Trenches events, loaned award-winning Hudswell Clarke G class No. 1238 of 1916, Motor-Rail Simplexes 40hp No. LR3090 and 20hp No. LR4978, and two First World War military wagons, a D class general service vehicle and an F class wagon.

Nothing to do with the Great War, but the showpiece event included the first public appearance of Britain's newest steam locomotive.

Duchess the shire horse hauling the D wagon during the Horses at War weekend. BEAMISH

Supplies on their way to the Front Line! BEAMISH

The museum's replica of Stephen Lewin 0-4-0WTG *Samson* was unveiled to the public in light steam with its flywheel turning over for the first time. Lewin's Poole Foundry, one of the more obscure British locomotive builders, supplied its second railway engine in 1874 to the London Lead Company for use on the mile-long Cornish Hush Mine tramway to the south of Weardale. It is believed that the locomotive was scrapped in 1904, and the only evidence that it existed are engravings, a photograph, and a description in the engineering press of the day.

Paul Jarman, assistant director of transport and industry at Beamish said: "This has been a spectacular commemoration of the men and women, and their machines, who played a largely

Local troops marching through Beamish town past tramcar No. 264, one of 15 double-deck balcony cars delivered in 1907 to Sheffield Corporation Tramways by the United Electric Car Company of Preston. BEAMISH

Members of a cavalry regiment patrol the borders of Beamish museum. BEAMISH

unsung role in supporting the fighting troops throughout the years of conflict, 1914 to 1918."

The Great War Steam Fair marked the start of this year's Great War Festival of Transport, which also featured Horses at War on April 16-17 and Old King Coal from April 20-24.

The Horses at War event focused on the use of horses in the First World War, and accordingly a War Department Light Railways' depot 'somewhere in France' was set up for military wagon shunting demonstrations.

Many visitors said they would return for the next Beamish First World War event on July 1-3, held as part of national commemorations to mark the centenary of the Battle of the Somme.

WAR
in the valley

It has been said that in Britain today, the two most popular historical subjects are railways and the Second World War – so what happens when the two meet in the middle? Answer – hugely popular Forties and wartime weekends on heritage railways all over the country – and one of the biggest and best is held each summer on the Severn Valley Railway.

Many of today's heritage railways have for years held phenomenally popular Forties or wartime weekends, some featuring hundreds of re-enactors, reprising roles ranging from Army officers and medical staff to shopkeepers and spivs. The archetypal characters of a bygone but fondly remembered era are brought back to life in droves. Many lines have found that Forties weekends prove more popular even than their eagerly anticipated enthusiast galas.

One of the market leaders in terms of Forties events is the Severn Valley Railway.

Over two weekends, normally at the end of June and the beginning of July, armies of re-enactors turn up in period costume, several with cars and military vehicles from the era.

Many of the visitors also dress up for the occasion to look the part. Period clothes stalls at Kidderminster and at Bewdley sell suits, dresses, trousers and hats, nowadays specially made for the growing Forties interest market. The 2015 event saw more than 7100 people descend on the railway to soak up the nostalgic atmosphere.

Among the familiar faces regularly re-

created for the event have been Sir Winston Churchill, King George VI and General Montgomery.

Thousands of people turn out to see the displays, exhibitions, entertainers and mock battle at Highley, as an intensive service of evacuation trains is timetabled. Visitors can gain a real insight into wartime life with replica air-raid shelters, bombed-out buildings, an ARP post, a Dig for Victory garden and privy, an ID card checkpoint and hospital train, as well as displays of historic civilian and military vehicles. Ladies can also head to the hair

A station platform bench was a brilliant place to meet people from diverse walks of life in the dark days of wartime. SVR

Never mind Hitler – the dog has to come too!

Donate your saucepans to the Spitfire Fund at Kidderminster Town station. JIM CARTER

Forties fashions are the order of the day over both weekends of the Severn Valley's summer wartime event. ANDY BISHOP/SVR

Patriotic crowds and bunting welcome GWR 4-6-0 No. 7812 *Bradley Manor* into Arley station. JOHN WRIGHT/SVR

"We'll meet again". A parting farewell as this soldier heads out to Front-Line duty. SVR

salon at Kidderminster to have their Victory Rolls done.

Musical performers get people 'in the mood' and a range of stalls selling Forties memorabilia are set up along the line.

Scheduled for the 2016 event is the sight of a group of children evacuated from their school in Bewdley taken by vintage bus to Kidderminster before going on to Bridgnorth by steam train on June 25-26 and on Saturday, July 2.

Visitors can also join the congregation at a Forties wedding, taking place at Arley each day.

Each station has its own attraction. Past events have seen Bewdley station yard host a display of family cars of the Thirties and Forties era and the story of wartime US Army Hospitals in an exhibition inside a Red Cross coach under the banner of Wyre Forest at War. Arley has been the site of the tented headquarters of a full Dad's Army platoon in the form of the Pitsford (Northants) Home Guard, which was

Bulleid Battle of Britain Pacific No. 34053 *Sir Keith Park* passes Oldbury Viaduct on September 30, 2015. Built after the war, it is named after the Air Vice-Marshall who is credited with victory in the Battle of Britain. LEWIS MADDOX

formed in 2005 as a tribute to the county's 9th (Brixworth) Batallion of the Northants Home Guard.

Station windows are taped up with blackout curtains and sandbags are laid around ARP posts, as the line becomes one giant film set – but one in which any member of the public can take part.

Passengers are issued with identity cards, copied from the genuine wartime design, and they have to produce them if asked by military or plain-clothes police.

Bakelite radios boom out BBC Home Service bulletins, 78rpm record-playing phonographs are wound up to play Glenn Miller 'big band sound' favourites from loudspeakers, and stalls selling all kinds of Forties memorabilia are positioned at stations along the line. On Kidderminster's concourse, spivs sell black market nylon stockings, chocolate and other unattainables from their battered suitcases.

The events have included flypasts over

Bewdley by the Battle of Britain Memorial Flight based at Coningsby in Lincolnshire and static displays of wartime aircraft, plus a convoy of historic and military vehicles going from Kidderminster to Arley.

Highlights have included simulated Luftwaffe bombing raids over Kidderminster Town station, with pyrotechnic 'explosions' and surround-sound recordings of bombers around the site.

In 2011, an RAF Lancaster bomber – one of only two in the world still airworthy – made two low-level passes over the railway, one in each direction.

Kidderminster station becomes a living museum of the Forties, with its own resident compere Guy Roles from Stourport, playing the big-band numbers of the age.

Visitors can experience life 'at home' in wartime with a three-sided mock-up of a typical terraced house of the period.

Its living room has flowery wallpaper and frumpy curtains, a horsehair sofa and oak sideboard with mantel clock and framed sepia photographs.

The sparse kitchen has a stone sink, a mangle and a washboard, an old Hoover and a gas stove or cooker. Re-enactors play family members peeling potatoes and boiling the kettle to make the tea.

The set even has a Dig For Victory allotment garden.

Visitors can take refuge during bombing raids in a corrugated steel Anderson shelter and also view the smaller, table-like self-assembly Morrison shelter, designed to absorb the impact of falling debris in homes without cellars.

The main attraction for many visitors is to be found at Highley, where the traditional 'battle' between German and Allied troops takes place around 1pm, aided by pyrotechnic effects and blank ammunition. The Engine House museum

Sunday best: all dressed up for an outing in the family car. SVR

"It's all one big adventure – and we're going by train into the bargain!" Evacuated children head to the safety of the Shropshire hills. SVR

Home on leave: a typical Forties interior. JIM CARTER

A gun emplacement and military fuel supplies at the ready. JIM CARTER

LEFT: George Formby did not have it all his own way – the ladies now get in on the act too! JOHN WRIGHT/SVR

Ladies pass the time while waiting for the next train. SVR

ARP notice signifying blackout times. JOHN WRIGHT/SVR

A Jeep in action at Highley. JIM CARTER

Youngsters get behind the wheel of a military vehicle. ANDY BISHOP/SVR

Trains fascinated youngsters just as much in the Forties as they do today. SVR

"We shall fight them on the beaches" – even though the Severn Valley Railway is landlocked without a bucket and space in sight! JOHN WRIGHT/SVR

Visitors inspect a Forties caravan.

"Winston Churchill" aka re-enactor Stan Streather arrives to deliver a morale-boosting speech to the troops, usually delivered at Highley at 1pm each day. JIM CARTER

Army officers chat to a footplateman on GWR 0-6-0 pannier tank No. 7714 before a morning departure. SVR

"Get me to the church on time!" A Forties wedding re-enacted. JIM CARTER

Ladies take over the running of trains while the menfolk are on forces duties. SVR

"Read all about it" – newspapers were a lifeline for war-weary Britons anxious for every glimmer of hope that the conflict might be turning their way. SVR

Soldiers guard Arley signalbox. JIM CARTER

and visitor centre becomes a live RAF wartime operations room.

Visitors are transported back to two days after the D-Day landings; paratroopers have been dropped behind enemy lines, their mission: to attack an enemy ammunition train. Will the Allies be able to destroy the dangerous, explosive-filled train, or will the enemy resistance prove too much?

Here, as at other heritage railways throughout Britain, SS uniforms and the portrayal of senior Nazi figures such as Hitler and Himmler have been banned, in line with Heritage Railway Association guidelines, for fear of causing offence. The sight of SS guards standing next to a line of general-purpose box vans ('cattle trucks' as such were rarely used on Nazi deportation trains) would have been the last that millions of their victims saw before arriving at death camps.

Thankfully, no German officer was ever seen standing next to a railway station on mainland Britain during the conflict, so any depiction otherwise would be wholly inaccurate.

The GWR Severn Valley route between Shrewsbury and Hartlebury Junction was never a big moneyspinner, linking as it did just a string of otherwise unrelated towns and villages along the river. Freight traffic, mostly agricultural, and coal traffic from the collieries at Alveley and Highley were the principal sources of revenue, and the growth of motor traffic following the First World War saw the writing slowly appear on the wall for this line and so many other country routes.

However, the line played a significant role in the Second World War. The cross-country route became a strategic bypass around Birmingham and the Black Country for troop and munitions trains.

During the conflict, the GWR's 51XX class large prairie tanks appeared on the line. Other strangers to the usual array of motive power included Cambrian Railways' 0-6-0s and J25 0-6-0s on loan from the LNER.

Several passenger trains were headed by vintage Duke class 4-4-0s, alongside Bulldog 4-4-0s, of which No. 3353 *Pershore Plum*, No. 3453 *Seagull* and No. 3454 *Skylark* became regular wartime visitors.

Sadly, we don't have any Bulldogs and Dukes left, but one of the big stars of wartime weekends in recent years has been a locomotive of a type that would never have been seen on the line in the Forties, but which carries the name of a man who made the Allied victory possible.

Bulleid Battle of Britain Pacific No. 34053 *Sir Keith Park*, is named after the New Zealand-born Air Chief Marshal nicknamed 'The Defender of London' who deployed Britain's squadrons of Hurricane and Spitfire fighters against the Luftwaffe in 1940.

The son of a Scottish geologist for a mining company, Keith Park was born on

GWR Bulldog 4-4-0 No. 3454 *Skylark* at Swindon, heads the Stephenson Locomotive Society (Midland Are) 'Bulldog Special' on June 17, 1951, which marked the last of the class in service. The trip ran from Birmingham Snow Hill to Swindon via Oxford and Didcot and back via the same route. The volunteer-led preservation movement at the time was just beginning, and sadly was light years away from being able to save a standard gauge locomotive like this. Many 'ancient' classes were given a breathing space from the scrapyard during the Second World War purely because of the locomotive shortage caused by demands for more trains. This Bulldog was one of several that could be regularly seen in passenger service along the Severn Valley route in those dark days. COLOUR-RAIL

June 15, 1892 in Thames on the Coromandel Peninsula.

He joined the Army as a Territorial soldier in the New Zealand Field Artillery but aged 19, he went to sea as a purser aboard collier and passenger steamships.

During the First World War, as a non-commissioned officer, he participated in the landings at Gallipoli in April 1915, and commanded an artillery battalion.During the conflict, he transferred from the New Zealand Army to the British Army, joining the Royal Horse and Field Artillery.

After Gallipoli, Park's battalion participated in the Battle of the Somme. On October 21, 1916, Park was blown off his horse by a German shell. Wounded, he was evacuated to England and medically certified 'unfit for active service' meaning he was unfit to ride a horse. So he joined the Royal Flying Corps in December 1916 and learned to fly.

He returned to France as a major to command 48 Squadron, and went on to earn a bar to his Military Cross, the Distinguished Flying Cross and the French Croix de Guerre.

When the new RAF officer ranks were introduced in 1919, Park became a Flight Lieutenant; promoted to Air Vice Marshal, Park took command of No. 11 Group RAF, responsible for the fighter defence of London and south-east England, in April 1940.

He organised fighter patrols over France during the Dunkirk evacuation and during the Battle of Britain his command took the full force of the Luftwaffe's air attacks.

Among the many air battles fought over Britain, Park personally commanded RAF forces on August 13 (Adlertag), August 18 (The Hardest Day) and September 15 (Battle of Britain Day).

Battle of Britain hero RAF pilot Douglas Bader said: "The awesome responsibility for this country's survival rested squarely on Keith Park's shoulders.

British military history of this century has been enriched with the names of great fighting men from New Zealand, of all ranks and in every one of our services. Keith Park's name is carved into history alongside those of his peers."

Park retired and was promoted to Air Chief Marshal on December 20, 1946 and returned to New Zealand, where was elected to Auckland City Council. He died on February 6, 1975, aged 82.

No. 34053 was built at Brighton Works in 1947, and allocated to Salisbury shed. Sir Keith himself named the engine on September 19, 1947, at Brighton station.

Following withdrawal in October 1965, No. 34053 arrived at Dai Woodham's scrapyard in Barry during March 1966.

It became the 153rd locomotive out of a total of 213 bought from the legendary scrapyard for preservation purposes, but ended up being resold to the multi-millionaire Jeremy Hosking as a source of spare parts for his West Country light Pacific No. 34046 *Braunton*.

Southern Locomotives bought the surplus-to-requirements remains of the locomotive in 2000 and moved them to its base at Sellindge in Kent, with the ultimate

aim of restoring it in its own right, as a memorial to the wartime hero.

Its restoration was completed in May 2012, and it was taken to the Severn Valley, which had agreed a long-term loan deal. It was rededicated at Kidderminster Town on August 31 in front of three RAF veterans who fought in the Battle of Britain, as well as members of Sir Keith's family and Oliver Bulleid, the grandson of the engine's designer.

The guest of honour was the Right Honourable Sir Lockward Smith, New Zealand High Commissioner, who unveiled the nameplate.

A guard of honour was mounted by the 156 (Kidderminster) Squadron ATC with a flypast by a Hurricane and a Spitfire from the Battle of Britain Memorial Flight taking place over Bridgnorth.

As a mark of respect to all of those who made the ultimate sacrifice, a bugler plays The Last Post, while the union flag will be lowered and prayers said in a short ceremony at Kidderminster Town station at around 4.30pm on both Sundays of the wartime weekends.

Clare Gibbard, the SVR's marketing and communications manager, said: "Our Forties weekends are always a huge hit with visitors who come back time and again to enjoy this all-encompassing celebration of the enduring spirit of wartime Britain."

* For bookings and more information on Forties weekends and other upcoming events and activities at the SVR, visit www.svr.co.uk, call 01562 757900.

The tube station from where the world was saved

A hidden part of London that contributed to the war effort

The front of long-closed Down Street station today. The surface building, designed by Leslie Green, was in the standard classical arts and crafts style adopted for most of the stations on the Great Northern, Piccadilly & Brompton Railway. The modern-day entrance to the old tube station, which became Churchill's bunker, is on the left of the Mayfair Mini shop. ROBIN JONES

RIGHT: The front of Down Street station as it appeared in July 1907, four months after it opened on March 17. The street was developed in the early 18th century by John Downes, whose family owned land and cottages in the area for several generations. LTM

The Mayfair Mini in Down Street Mews in the City of Westminster is one of those so convenient stores where you can buy a lunchtime sandwich or a soft drink, or maybe photocopy a document if needs be.

Those who are more in tune with the finer points of railway architecture will see that this little, but very useful store, occupied what would once have been the entrance to the booking hall of a tube station.

However, few would ever realise that a purely functional steel door to the side of the shop leads to a place, where world history may have been changed for the better.

This door leads to a spiral staircase, crucial to the war effort in the Second World War, which until 1932 took passengers down to the Piccadilly Line, that is, the few passengers who used Down Street station, rather than nearby Green Park or Hyde Park Corner, or even their own transport, as most wealthy Mayfair residents did. Yet that staircase leads to a far greater treasure than just any old abandoned tube station.

In historical terms, you might argue that what lies at the bottom is in its own way more important than anything you might find in Tutankhamun's tomb.

A ridiculous comparison you may think, when the great pharaoh's tomb was laden with treasures beyond belief, when down those stairs you will just find a sequence of tunnels and side rooms, with flaking paint and a few bits of obsolete electrical equipment.

Not so. Tutankhamun never saved the world. Yet that is exactly what may have happened well below street level in Down Street.

Down Street station was opened in 1907 by the Great Northern, Piccadilly & Brompton Railway, and was in its final years served by the Piccadilly line. However, patronage was poor, so much so that passing trains often missed it out.

The station closed as early as May 21, 1932, but its finest hour by far was yet to come. For the station was selected for use as a bombproof underground bunker in early 1939, as part of a programme developing deep shelters to protect government operations from bombing in the event of war.

In the mid-Thirties, Winston Churchill often found himself a lone voice at Westminster, warning about the rise of Nazi Germany. However, as black clouds increasingly thickened over the eastern horizon, others began to echo his concerns, to the point where the Chamberlain

Chris Nix, London Transport Museum's assistant director of collections and engagement, shows guests the interior of the bombproof rooms deep underground in Down Street station when Churchill and the Railway Executive Committee made key decisions that could impact on the future of the war. ROBIN JONES

This view, taken in the committee room at the Down Street Railway Executive Committee headquarters on April 26, 1940, shows (left to right): Sir Eustace J Missenden, (SR); Sir James Milne, (GWR deputy chairman); Sir William Wood, (LMSR); Mr WH Mills, (REC minute clerk); EG Marsden, (REC assistant to secretary); Sir Charles H Newton, (LNER); Frank Pick, (London Transport); Sir Ralph Wedgwood, LNER general manager (first REC chairman); G Cole Deacon, (REC secretary); and V M Barrington Ward (chairman of the Operating Committee). Decisions affecting the nation's railway in the Second World War were being made from a tube station that closed seven years before hostilities broke out. LTM

government – far from universally believing in 'peace for our time', began to prepare for the event of hostilities breaking out.

One of the contingency plans was to bring the nation's railways under state control, as happened during the First World War.

On September 24, 1938, the Railway Executive Committee was formed to coordinate British railway companies in the event of war and to ensure that the network would meet all military requirements.

The committee was based in Fielden House, Great College Street, Westminster, near the seat of government and comprised representatives from the Big Four companies along with the London Passenger Transport Board.

REC chairman Sir Ralph Wedgwood of the LNER wrote to the REC secretary G Cole Deacon, who came from the Railway Companies Association, recalling the problems encountered when the government ran the network during the First World War. He expressed his concerns about the growing possibilities of war and calling for the committee. He suggested that preparations should be made immediately to relocate to safer accommodation, maybe Guildford or Rickmansworth, to protect the REC telephone exchange, which would be crucial if the country came under attack.

Unlike the railway companies, which

were planning to move their headquarters out of London, the REC remained in the capital to stay in close contact with the government.

A basement in Fielden House – the first option to be considered in depth, was unsuitable – Scotland Yard warned of the flooding risk and the building's vulnerability to aerial attack and so disused Down Street was selected for conversion into bombproof underground

offices to house the REC headquarters. A formal lease with London Transport was signed on March 28, 1939, and the LMS drew up a blueprint for its conversion.

The only available space was on the platforms, but Piccadilly Line trains still passed through the station. Under great secrecy, new walls were built at night when the trains had stopped running.

The doors to the new headquarters were fitted with gas locks, air filtration and

The front of Camden station was damaged in an air raid during the Blitz of 1940. At the time, Churchill may have been safely underground in a tube station that had disappeared off the map eight years before! LTM

THE BLITZ

During the Blitz from September 1940 to March 1941, the amount of high explosive, incendiary bombs and parachute mines falling on Whitehall damaged 10 Downing Street such that Churchill had to move out while the building was repaired and strengthened. He stated that the War Cabinet's own shelter provision was unfit for purpose.

Work was underway to strengthen the Cabinet War Rooms, as they would not have been able to survive a direct hit from a large bomb.

In mid-October 1940, Josiah Wedgwood, brother of REC chairman Sir Ralph Wedgwood persuaded Churchill that the REC headquarters at Down Street would make the ideal shelter for him.

So, between October and December 1940, Churchill used Cole Deacon's office at Down Street as his sleeping quarters.

On November 19 that year, the prime minster dined there with members of the REC and the War Cabinet who were served caviar,

Perrier Jouet 1928 Champagne, 1865 brandy and fine cigars.

The next day, the War Cabinet formally asked London Transport to build the capital's public deep-level shelters on its behalf.

Churchill called Down Street 'The Barn', but he was so impressed by the REC's Down Street headquarters during the many nights he spent there, that he asked for special quarters for his own use to be provided there.

Despite reservations by London Transport engineers, that using the only spare passageway left free would cause problems with the use of the station for the ventilation of the Piccadilly Line, the work was approved on January 22, 1941, and was completed ahead of its six-week schedule.

However, it was all in vain, for by the time Churchill's personal quarters had been completed, the reinforcement of the Cabinet War Rooms was finished, and the Prime Minster had no further need for Down Street.

This tunnel was converted into a room where Winston Churchill would spend the night. He was here on November 19, 1940, a particularly bad night of the Blitz. ROBIN JONES

short, secret, platforms were added, from which REC members and senior staff could stop a train and travel in the cab to the next station.

The new headquarters included meeting rooms and offices, dormitories, dining facilities, kitchens, and mess rooms. The site was equipped with its own telephone exchange connected to 50 telephones and a Teletype machine, so it could send missives to the railway network.

The postal address of Down Street was kept secret, so post was taken to and from site by a dedicated team of four LT motorcycle dispatch riders who carried letters on a circuit between stations, head offices and government buildings.

The rooms were kitted out to a high standard by LMS carriage fitters, who plastered, painted or panelled over most of the original tiled walls.

Main offices and mess rooms were fitted with radio sets connected to a receiving aerial above ground.

REC staff worked shifts to provide continuous 24/7 operation, seven days a week. To avoid attracting attention with a constant stream of people entering a disused station, most staff were also required to live and sleep there. A total of 19 staff dormitory rooms were provided, eight of which accommodated three people in shared, tiered bunk beds.

Only the executive members of staff had bedrooms to themselves.

Catering was provided by a kitchen at platform level, serving a staff mess room and an executive mess room. Food came via the railway hotels and was of a good standard.

THE BOLTHOLE BELOW

The REC was able to carry out its vital duties throughout the war from Down Street, unbothered by air raids.

From there, it administered the movement of ambulance trains, food trains, munitions and personnel.

It also had to deal with matters big and small relating to the smooth running of the network in wartime, such as arranging for milk supplies to be rerouted, so that milk was not wasted when a railway line had been bombed, or whether directional notices telling passengers to keep to the left should include 'keep left' notices in French and Polish.

No bombs ever fell directly on Down Street, and so the effectiveness of its reinforced shielding was never tested.

The operation from the disused tube station was so successful that the REC stayed there after the war was over, not leaving until New Year's Eve 1947.

Hostilities over, the REC dispersed – its existence had gone a long way to supporting the case for the nationalisation of Britain's railways on January 1, 1948: unwanted and unloved Down Street station went back to its main prewar use as a giant ventilation shaft for the Piccadilly Line.

HIDDEN LONDON

by london transport museum

SEE INSIDE CHURCHILL'S SECRET HQ TODAY

Down Street tube station is one of the centrepieces of a new series of Hidden London tours organised by the award-winning London Transport Museum in Covent Garden.

Visitors are being invited to take light refreshments at the five-star Athenaeum Hotel in Mayfair's Down Street – before crossing the road to tour the long-abandoned Underground station opposite.

Visitors can descend its spiral staircase, which still has many of its wartime bunker signs in place, to the ghostly passages below, which remain a time capsule from when the REC finally left the bunker.

Peeling wallpaper, cracking plaster, the occasional path of soot and the remnants of Forties telephone equipment fill this most ghostly of Underground properties.

Guests will be able to return to the hotel after the tour for refreshments as an optional addition to the package. Michelin-star London chefs the Galvin brothers launched their new restaurant and bar at the Athenaeum in June,

The spiral staircase leading from street level down to the disused Down Street tube station and Churchill's secret wartime bunker complex. ROBIN JONES

Late 20th-century signs inside Down Street reflect the fact it can still be used as emergency access to the Piccadilly Line, for which it acts a giant ventilation shaft. ROBIN JONES

and as such are creating a special afternoon tea for Hidden London tour guests. The hotel was awarded Best Afternoon Tea in London 2012 by the Tea Guild.

In 2016, the Down Street tours were scheduled to run on Wednesdays, Thursdays, Fridays, Saturdays and Sundays, from August 4 to September 11; November 24 to December 18 and January 11 to March 5.

Corridors of power that were narrower than anything in the Whitehall of Churchill's day! ROBIN JONES

The room used as a kitchen where top chefs would prepare meals for Churchill and his cabinet, which would be delivered by silver service waiters. ROBIN JONES

The remains of the telephone exchange inside the station. ROBIN JONES

Ancient tile signs from the earliest days of Down Street station. ROBIN JONES

Wartime signage, which has stood the test of time, points to way to Churchill's underground headquarters. ROBIN JONES

This gas-tight door added further protection to Churchill's bunker. ROBIN JONES

A locked grille separates Down Street station from the modern Piccadilly Line. ROBIN JONES

ABOVE AND RIGHT: Original tiling from Down Street survived both its wartime conversion and decades of mothballing afterwards. ROBIN JONES

The front of the Clapham South deep shelter in 1955. TfL

SEE INSIDE THE CLAPHAM SOUTH WARTIME BUNKER TOO

A second venue in the 2016 Hidden London programme is the deep shelter at Clapham South.

With the clouds of war looming, contingency plans were made to safeguard as much of London's population from air raids as possible.

Ten massive underground shelters, each capable of holding 8000 people were planned.

Each shelter consists of a pair of parallel tunnels 1200ft long and 16ft 6in in diameter. Each tunnel was subdivided into two decks, and each shelter was designed to hold up to 8000 people.

The intention was that after the war the shelters would be used as part of new express tube lines paralleling parts of the existing Northern and Central lines, and capable of being used by main line trains – a form of early Crossrail might-have-been.

Only eight of the planned 10 shelters were completed: at Chancery Lane station on the Central Line and Belsize Park, Camden Town, Goodge Street, Stockwell, Clapham North, Clapham Common and Clapham South on the Northern Line.

Building work began in in 1940 and the shelters were ready in 1942.

They were originally all used by the government, but as bombing intensified five of them were opened to the public in 1944: Stockwell, Clapham North, Camden Town, Belsize Park and Clapham South.

In 1948, the Clapham South shelter, which has more than a mile of subterranean passageways reached by 180 steps, was used to house the first immigrants from the West Indies who had arrived on the *MV Empire Windrush*. In 1951, it accommodated hard-up visitors to the Festival of Britain who could not afford proper accommodation.

The Goodge Street shelter was used by General Eisenhower, and the Chancery Lane

London Transport Museum's Hidden London tours take visitors through the deep shelter tunnels at Clapham South. TfL

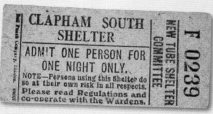

Clapham South deep shelter blue ticket. LTM

Clapham South deep shelter red ticket. LTM

The Clapham South Air Raid Precautions room in 1944. PLANET NEWS/ LTM

Red Cross nurses in the Clapham South shelter sick bay, 1944. PLANET NEWS/LTM

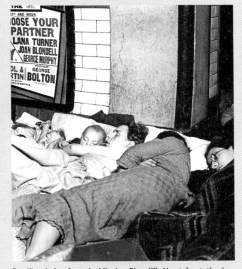

Families shelter from the blitz in a Piccadilly Line tube station in 1940. LTM

Clapham South deep-level shelter exit staircase and lift, as seen in 1942. TOPICAL PRESS/ LTM

shelter became a communications centre.

After the war, the Goodge Street shelter continued to be used by the Army until the Fifties, and the Chancery Lane shelter was converted into a Kingsway telephone exchange, as well as being expanded to serve as a Cold War government shelter.

The Clapham North shelter was purchased in 2014 by the Zero Carbon Food Company, which uses the shelter as a hydroponic farm.

The Clapham South tours are scheduled to run in 2016 on Wednesdays, Thursdays, Fridays, Saturdays and Sundays, from July 14 to August 21, and March 2-26, 2017.

Two other Hidden London tours are on offer in the 2016 programme – the lost tunnels beneath Euston station and Grade I listed 55 Broadway at St James's Park, London's first skyscraper when it was built in 1929, and the headquarters of London Underground until recently.

* For further details about all of the Hidden London tours, including times, dates and prices, visit ltmuseum.co.uk/hiddenlondon

For details of the afternoon tea package at the Athenaeum Hotel visit www.athenaeumhotel.com

Inside the Clapham South shelter tunnels today. TfL

The world's smallest military railway!

Many heritage railways stage Forties or wartime weekends, with re-enactors reprising the life and times of Britain's darkest days. Yet only one can claim to having run genuine Second World War military trains.

The Romney Hythe & Dymchurch Railway long claimed to be the world's smallest public railway, its 15in gauge locomotives and stock running on a 'main line in miniature'.

Running for 13½ miles from Hythe to Dungeness, it was created by racing driver, millionaire landowner, former Army officer and miniature-railway fan Captain Jack Howey and Count Louis Zborowski, a wealthy aristocrat who was also famous as a racing driver.

Zborowski wanted to build a fully working express railway in miniature. The locomotives would be scale replicas of main line steam locomotives, but would run on 15in gauge, not 4ft 8½in.

The pair tried in vain to buy the Ravenglass & Eskdale Railway in the Lake District, a 15in gauge line that in 1915 had

been laid on the trackbed of an earlier 3ft-gauge freight operation.

Undeterred, Zborowski ordered two Pacific locomotives to be designed by the leading model railway engineer of his day, Henry Greenly, to be built in Colchester by Davey, Paxman and Co, in anticipation of the day the pair would have a railway of their own on which to run them. They were named *Green Goddess*, after the 1921 stage play by William Archer, which Howey had enjoyed, and *Northern Chief*.

However, Zborowski died while racing at Monza in the Italian Grand Prix before they could be delivered.

Captain Howey was left with the two locomotives and finding a line on which to run them. Henry Greenly came up with the idea of building a railway along the coast of Romney Marsh.

A double-track line was laid over the eight miles along the English Channel coast between Hythe and New Romney, the railway's headquarters, and the official opening took place on July 16, 1927, with another Pacific, Hercules, hauling the first train.

Howey extended the double tracks to Dungeness via Greatstone the following year.

The line was billed as the 'Smallest Public Railway in the World' and proved enormously popular. Soon there were nine miniature versions of main line express Pacific engines hauling a fleet of luxurious coaches.

The railway is still very much with us, as part of Britain's proud portfolio of heritage lines, and a major contributor to the nation's tourist economy.

Davey Paxman 4-8-2 No. 5 *Hercules* in a very different form to that which its builders intended in 1926 – as the centrepiece of a military train defending the Kent coast against the Nazi menace. It is seen passing a bomb crater at Dymchurch. RHDR

COMETH THE HOUR, COMETH THE MINIATURE RAILWAY...

Any notion that the Romney Hythe & Dymchurch was a 'toy' rather than 'real' railway were dispelled during the Second World War, when it found itself in the front line of Britain's defence.

Just as the Royal Military Canal had been built across the northern edge of Romney Marsh in 1810 to provide a line of defence should Napoleon's troops have landed, so the little railway that ran just over 20 miles over the water from northern France found itself pressed into Army service.

It was requisitioned by the Army on June 15, 1940 and much of the area was evacuated of all but essential persons. This part of the Kent coast effectively became the front line... and the Somerset Light infantry took over the railway. Within the battalion were several railwaymen including "two shunting drivers, two firemen and enough ex-railwaymen of other grades to make up a railway detachment."

The War Department created the only miniature railway armoured train in the world as the line was used for patrols of the coast by the 6th Battalion of the Somerset Light Infantry commanded by Col DIL Beath and with extensive transport of soldiers on troop trains.

Guns at the ready as an enemy aircraft approaches the Kent coast. RHDR

Davey Paxman 4-62- No. 1 *Green Goddess* in 1925 became the first Romney Hythe & Dymchurch Railway locomotive and is still very much active today. DEREK PRITCHARD/RHDR

Yet it is a heritage railway purely by default. It predates the volunteer-run Talyllyn Railway by nearly a quarter of a century. The Talyllyn is regarded as the world's first heritage line after transport historian Tom Rolt saved it from closure in 1951.

When the Ravenglass & Eskdale, and Romney Hythe & Dymchurch lines were created, they were not preserving anything, but running new locomotives and stock decades before there was a need to save steam locomotives for posterity, and their primary purpose was as commercial passenger-carrying lines, if only for pleasure purposes.

The armoured train passes Dymchurch signalbox. RHDR

Hercules with the armoured train at Dymchurch. RHDR

A wartime locomotive crew take a breather. RHDR

Hercules on a routine coastal patrol. RHDR

Romney, Hythe & Dymchurch Railway wartime railway staff. RHDR

Immediately following the requisition, the section between New Romney and Hythe was used for battalion transport, carrying leave parties to and from Hythe, collecting incoming troops off main line trains and performing such essential journeys as conveying laundry.

The little railways filled a useful role in transporting people and supplies at a time when petrol was in very short supply.

The tea room at Dymchurch station became their headquarters (that sounds like a plot from Dad's Army!) while local holiday camps were used as barracks for all the soldiers stationed in the area.

To provide the railway with at least a small element of firepower, the battalion officers thought up the idea of an armoured train, and Woolwich Arsenal and the Southern Railway's Ashford Works converted the idea into a reality.

This unique military train emerged in the summer of 1940 as a 'three-car' unit, with No. 5 Hercules sandwiched between two bogie hopper wagons.

All were clad in mild steel boiler plate to provide some protection against small arms fire and the wagons additionally had concrete screening at vital points.

Each wagon was fitted with two Lewis light machine guns and a Boys anti-tank rifle – not particularly effective, but all that was available.

The Somersets were relieved in October 1940 by the 4th Battalion of the Royal West Kents who seemingly did not have the same interest or maybe expertise in running a railway.

Fortunately the Royal Engineers took over from them in 1941 and its RE Railway Company managed the line to a very high standard.

As well as front line defence and troop trains, the line was also used for training.

Luftwaffe pilots would regularly drop any leftover bombs from London air raids over Kent on their way back to base.

On one occasion a German pilot spotted a train near Dymchurch and he dropped several bombs in its direction.

One fell just ahead of the train, which fell into the resulting crater. The locomotive (Black Prince) was renamed Winston Churchill in 1948 - could this be a case of Adolf bombing Winnie?

It has often been speculated that the pilot from the air couldn't tell that this was a miniature train rather than a full size one, but we will probably never know...

No Jerries will get past the Romney, Hythe & Dymchurch Railway's armoured train! RHDR

The Romney, Hythe & Dymchurch Railway's armoured train patrolled one of the nearest sections of British mainland coast to Nazi-occupied Europe. RHDR

THE LAYING OF PLUTO

The railway was also used extensively during the building of PLUTO (Pipe Line Under The Ocean), which fuelled the Allied invasion force following the D-Day landings on June 5, 1944.

Operation Pluto was a combined operation involving British engineers, oil companies and armed forces to construct temporary undersea oil pipelines beneath the English Channel between England and France in support of Operation Overlord, the Allied invasion of Normandy on D-Day.

The innovative scheme was developed by Arthur Hartley, the chief engineer with the Anglo-Iranian Oil Company.

Allied forces on the European continent would need a tremendous amount of fuel. Pipelines were considered necessary to relieve dependence on oil tankers, which could be slowed by bad weather, were susceptible to U-boat attacks, and were also needed in the Pacific war.

Geoffrey William Lloyd the minister for petroleum, met Admiral Mountbatten, chief of combined operations, in 1942 and adopted Hartley's idea of using adapted submarine telephone cable.

A full-scale rehearsal using a 2in diameter pipe took place between December 26-30, 1942, a 30-mile pipeline being laid across the Bristol Channel, in very bad and rough weather, and the shore ends being connected up at Swansea and Ilfracombe. It proved so successful that a 3in diameter pipe was considered, cutting the number of pipelines needed to pump the planned volume of petrol across the channel.

The PLUTO pipelines were linked to pump stations on the English coast, housed in various inconspicuous buildings including cottages and garages. Though uninhabited, these were intended to cloak the real purpose of the buildings. Pluto Cottage at Dungeness, a pumping station built to look like a small house, is now a

A cable drum used for the PLUTO pipeline laying is carried on a Romney, Hythe & Dymchurch Railway well wagon. RHDR

bed and breakfast. PLUTO was supplied by a 1000-mile network of pipelines that had been laid at night to prevent detection by aerial reconnaissance.

The first line to France was laid on August 12, 1944, over 70 nautical miles from Shanklin Chine on the Isle of Wight to Cherbourg.

By January 1945, 305 tons of fuel was being pumped to France each day, increasing to 3048 tons by March, and eventually to 4000 tons (nearly a million gallons) per day.

Dumbo was the codename given to the PLUTO pipeline that ran across Romney Marsh to Dungeness and then across the

to France. Its route can still be traced in various places on Romney Marsh. Where the pipeline crossed water drainage ditches, it ran above ground in a concrete case, and several of these can still be found.

As the fighting moved closer to Germany, 17 other lines were laid from Dungeness to Ambleteuse in the Pas-de-Calais. Along with the Mulberry harbours that were constructed immediately after D-Day, Operation Pluto remains one of the most ingenious and successful feats of military engineering of all time. The pipelines are also the forerunners of all flexible pipes used in the development of offshore oilfields.

A section of PLUTO pipe.

Laying the PLUTO pipeline: a 'conundrum' (Cone-ended drum, a purpose-designed piece of pipe-laying apparatus), is moved into position into a specially constructed dock in preparation for the winding on of the pipe. IMPERIAL WAR MUSEUM

The acoustic mirrors at Denge: left to right, the 200ft, 20ft and 30ft mirrors. A short branch of the Romney, Hythe & Dymchurch Railway carried the raw materials to build them. JK SOLOMON*

LISTENING FOR THE ENEMY

The Second World War, however, was not the first time that the Romney Hythe & Dymchurch Railway had been used for military purposes.

In 1929, at the request of the War Office, a branch line was constructed, curving away inland from a point south of Romney Sands station, which was then then known as Maddieson's Camp. The branch provided a train service to a secret RAF installation working on acoustic aircraft detection at Denge.

The site chosen is about half a mile inland from the shore. There were no roads anywhere near the site at the time so the miniature railway, which opened in 1928, was the obvious choice to carry all the building materials needed. The short single-line branch trailing away from the Up or Hythe-bound line was installed.

The War Department had its own small locomotive, built on a four-wheel wagon chassis and powered by an Austin 7 engine, and a two-road shed was built alongside Hythe turntable to house it. It had running

rights for the full length of the railway. Over the years, it underwent many changes of body, and it is the only independently owned locomotive to have ever seen long-term service on the railway. Daily military staff trains ran between Hythe station and the end of the branch.

The branch ended at an informal terminus known as War Department Halt, the location of which is believed to have moved several times during its 15 years of operation. It was never an official station and no platform or shelter was ever provided.

Anecdotal stories talk of trains stopping at the junction points to pick up and set down staff, who would then have to walk the last part on foot.

The Denge site housed a series of concrete acoustic 'mirrors', colloquially known as 'listening ears.' Developed by Dr William Sansome Tucker, they were built in the late Twenties as an experimental early-warning system to detect incoming aircraft.

The site contains three mirrors, one 200ft, one 30ft and one 20ft. Several mirrors were built along the south and east coasts, but the complex at Denge is the best preserved.

We might consider them eccentric inventions today, but acoustic mirrors did detect slow-moving aircraft before they came into sight. They worked by concentrating sound waves towards a central point, where a microphone would have been located. The listening ears could hear planes coming from about 20 miles away, as long as they were directly in front of the ears.

As housing developed along the seafront after the coast road was built, the peace and quiet of the locality was shattered, further reducing the viability of the whole project.

As aircraft became faster, their value diminished, and operators also found it difficult to distinguish between aircraft and seagoing vessels.

Meanwhile, Cpt Howey had been trying for years to secure privilege rate travel for his staff on the main line railways including the Southern Railway. He had already extended this privilege to SR staff travelling on the RHDR.

The SR in 1936-37 were in the process of diverting its branch from Lydd Town to New Romney with the intention of opening two new stations at Lydd-on-Sea and Greatstone-on-Sea.

This new line crossed the path of the War Department siding and a level junction was proposed. However, an objection was received from the local military advisor.... who was none other than Cpt Howey!

He insisted that a bridge over the line was installed. The SR duly obliged with a double-track bridge even though its line was single. The 15in gauge line had to be lowered several feet to save too big a hump in the standard gauge line, making a difficult train even harder to work.

The sound mirrors experiment finally came to an end in 1938. Radar was invented in 1932, and following a series of successful

The microphone housing in one of the Denge acoustic mirrors survives. RHDR

The War Department's scooter-like locomotive, which was provided for running over the Denge branch pictured in 1947. By this time it was in use by the permanent way gang. RHDR

By 1950, the War Department locomotive had a makeshift cab. A major rebuild followed in the early Sixties and it was again rebuilt in 1974-75. The arrival of two diesels on the line made 'The Scooter' as it is now known redundant, but it is kept in working order and makes very occasional journeys, although the sole-surviving original part is said to be the gear differential. RHDR

experiments, the mirrors were abandoned.

Around 1935 a company (partly owned by Cpt Howey and the railway) was set up to extract shingle from around the area. The ballast was transported in skips to Hythe, where bunkers and an unloading ramp were installed. The Denge branch was used in this operation.

No. 5 *Hercules* was mainly used as motive power and as the trains had to run outside the passenger train hours, they would often have to run during the hours of darkness. *Hercules* was fitted with a powerful headlight with a Kohler generator and batteries mounted either side of the running plate just ahead of the firebox.

The unbraked skips proved quite a handful with a high centre of gravity. Initially the tubs had no holes in them, so if it rained they would fill up with water, which then would freeze and occasionally topple over, sometimes pulling other skips with them! By the late Forties the gravel working was cut back to New Romney, initially unloading was done using a temporary ramp in the area that is now a car park. After that a crushing plant

was installed alongside the line on the Dungeness branch, with a purpose-built ramp and siding being installed there. Again sadly I am not aware of any pictures.

In 1947 Cpt Howey purchased the rolling stock from the defunct Eaton Hall Railway including a petrol-engined Simplex locomotive.

This locomotive took over the ballast workings until 1951 when the economics proved too costly and lorries replaced trains, and the branch to the once-secret but very obsolete acoustic mirrors was closed and lifted. Nowadays, the site of War Department Halt is said to be several feet under water in a gravel pit.

In 2003, English Heritage secured £500,000 from the Aggregates Levy Sustainability Fund and from the EU's Interreg programme under the Historic Fortifications Network to restore and preserve the sound mirrors.

BELOW: The acoustic mirrors as seen from the bridge that carried the Southern Railways' New Romney branch over the Romney, Hythe & Dymchurch Railway military branch to Denge. RHDR

A close-up view of the 200ft mirror. RHDR

The 200ft sound mirror shortly after the project was abandoned. RHDR

No. 5 *Hercules* at Ashford Works alongside Bulleid West Country light Pacific No. 21C119 *Bideford* in 1946. RHDR

A FINE MESS THEY GOT ME INTO…

The Romney Hythe & Dymchurch Railway was handed back to its owner after the end of the war, and the Hythe to New Romney section re-opened to the public in 1946. Several of its locomotives including *Hercules* were sent to Ashford Works for overhaul.

The Southern Railway also built four tenders for the engines. The first was attached to *Hercules*, but after a mix up, it was built over height, possibly to match the two Canadian-style locomotives at the RHDR.

Hercules duly had its cab roof raised to match, but it never looked right and was eventually cut back down again.

Italian prisoners of war were used to make good the damage to the railway that it had suffered during the war years.

The Romney to Dungeness section was reopened a year later with no less than Hollywood comedy giants Laurel and Hardy cutting the ribbon.

However, the war years had taken their toll,

and the New Romney to Dungeness section had been reduced to single line only, as the raw materials to rebuild were scarce and the cost of reinstatement enormous.

With the growth of tourism along the Kent coast in the Fifties and Sixties, the railway greatly benefited, but as cheap package holidays abroad became readily available, fewer holidaymakers came and receipts fell.

Cpt Howey died in September 1963 with the lack of investment in the line already evident, a problem not fully addressed by subsequent owners. The rolling stock was ageing and giving rough rides, the locomotives were costly to maintain and ridges were in poor condition.

Multi-millionaire enthusiast Sir William McAlpine, who once owned LNER A3 Pacific No. 4472 *Flying Scotsman*, and who has a private standard gauge railway of his own at his Fawley Hill home near Henley-on-Thames, stepped in to reverse the downward trend in 1973, and since then, the railway has gone from strength to strength.

A main line should have a grand terminus, and in 1974, a new trainshed was erected over the New Romney platforms to give the impression of a major city terminus.

The fleet expanded in 1976 with German-built locomotive No. 11 *Black Prince*, while all 10 original locomotives remain in service, covering thousands of miles each year. As well as the nine Pacifics and 4-8-2s, there was Krauss 0-4-0 tender tank locomotive No. 4, which left the railway in 1926 after construction and ran in Belfast with the new name *Jean*. It returned to Romney was restored, and is known as *The Bug*. There are now a total of 16 locomotives.

Not only is the line a major tourist attraction,

Laurel and Hardy were the VIP guests at the Re-opening of the line to Dungeness in 1947. ROBIN JONES COLLECTION

Its armour plating removed, *Hercules* with driver Terry Holder in charge heads a standard service train at New Romney in 1947. RHDR

In 1989 a replica (wooden rather than steel plate) armoured train was constructed – and at first powered, like the original, by *Hercules*. It can often be seen on static display usually at New Romney. RHDR

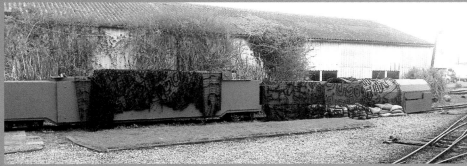

The replica armoured train at New Romney on May 10, 2013. RHDR

but also provides a public service between the small towns and villages between Hythe and Dungeness.

It is under contract to the local council to transport children to and from The Marsh Academy in New Romney. Local residents are transported to shopping centres and the railway

has operated 'shoppers specials'. Holiday camp trains have operated with campers at Romney Sands and St Mary's Bay.

Since 1982, the 10¼ in gauge Wells & Walsingham Light Railway in North Norfolk, laid along part of the Great Eastern Railway's Wells-next-the-Sea branch, has claimed the title

of world's smallest public railway.

*My thanks to Andrew Nash, historian of the Romney Hythe & Dymchurch Railway Heritage Association, for his help in compiling this chapter.

BELOW: The entire modern-day steam fleet lines up outside the shed at New Romney. RHDR

STANIER 8Fs
wartime workhorses for home and abroad

Whereas the designated standard heavy freight locomotive in the First World War was the Great Central Railway's Robinson 8K, during the Second World War, that honour went to William Stanier's LMS 8F 2-8-0, one of the most popular and successful of all British main lines types.

The Stanier 8F was, in effect, a freight version of the designer's go-anywhere, do-anything LMS 'Black Five' 4-6-0s, which were largely based on the GWR Hall class. The first appeared in 1934 and the last of 842 in 1951.

Examples were in service on the last day of British Railways standard gauge steam haulage on August 11, 1968, and they were a firm favourite among both drivers and enthusiasts.

The design of the 8F started out as a response to the Midland Railway's small engine policy, which basically had led to 0-6-0s doubleheading the heavier trains, a waste of manpower and resources.

Stanier's 8F design incorporated the two-cylinder arrangement of the Black Fives. They were initially classified 7F, but this was later changed to the more familiar 8F.

When the 8F was selected as Britain's standard freight design at the start of the Second World War, the War Department requisitioned 51 Crewe and Vulcan Foundry-built examples and ordered 208 from Beyer Peacock and North British Production. This continued until 1943, when the first of Robert Riddles' cheaper WD Austerity 2-8-0s appeared.

The Railway Executive Committee ordered Stanier 8Fs to be built at the works of three of the Big Four companies, excluding the LMS.

The GWR's Swindon Works turned out 80 as did LNER's Darlington Works. The LNER's Doncaster Works produced 30, while the Southern Railway built 23 at Eastleigh, 14 at Ashford and 68 at Brighton, all on REC orders.

For the LNER, which classified them O6, Brighton built 25, the company's own

Darlington Works 23 and Doncaster 20. Production for use on the national network as opposed to military purposes continued until 1946.

The War Department originally ordered Stanier 8Fs for service in support of the British Expeditionary Force, but they were not ready until after Dunkirk and the surrender of France.

However, they were shipped to Egypt, Palestine, Iran and Italy for military purposes, mostly as kits of parts to be assembled when they reached their destinations, and after the war, many were sold to these countries' railways. Turkey and Iraq also bought examples.

Famously, two were lost when Luftwaffe bombs sunk British armed Merchant Navy ship the SS *Thistlegorm* on October 6, 1941 near Ras Muhammad in the Red Sea.

Stanier 8Fs were at first used by the

Stanier 8F No. 8624 is the sole-surviving Southern Railway-built example. Built for wartime needs at Ashford Works in 1943, it was restored to working order in 2009 by Peak Rail in fictional LMS crimson lake livery as No. 8624, and is now based at the Great Central Railway as No. 48624 in British Railways' livery. It is seen heading a mineral wagon train from Loughborough Central station on January 29, 2016. The last-surviving LNER-built example, 1944-built No. 48518, and one of the last 10 locomotives to leave Barry scrapyard, it was used as a parts donor for the Great Western Society's new-build Hawksworth 4-6-0 No. 1014 *County of Glamorgan* and new LMS Patriot 4-6-0 No. 45551 *The Unknown Warrior*. PAUL LUCAS*

LEFT: Stanier 8F No. 48773 at the front of a rake of GWR stock at Bewdley in 1987. BRIAN SHARPE

Stanier 8F No. 48431 is the only-surviving Second World War Swindon-built example. Dating from 1944, it is displayed in the Keighley & Worth Valley Railway's exhibition shed at Oxenhope station. ROBIN JONES

British Army's Middle East Forces in Egypt, on the Western Desert Extension Railway. However, lack of water in the desert hampered the operation of steam locomotives, and smoke from them gave their locations away to enemy aircraft, a reason for the use of Motor-Rail Simplexes during the First World War. Late in 1942, they were replaced by US diesels.

Eventually, the Middle East Forces' 8F fleet totalled 90. After the war ended, 39 were sold in 1948 to the new British Railways, and five were brought home in 1952 for War Department use.

Following the occupation of Iran in 1941, WD locomotives were required to operate the Persian Corridor supply route, delivering war materials to the Soviet Union via the Trans-Iranian Railway. For this purpose, 163 Stanier 8Fs were sent to Iran in 1941-42, but only 143 arrived, with a dozen lost at sea and eight being returned to the UK having been damaged during shipping.

In Persia, 8Fs operated as Iranian State Railways' Class 41s, but many became redundant when the US Army Transportation Corps brought in diesels, which again were more suited to the desert conditions.

Stanier 8Fs ran in Iran until by 1963, while 12 were sold to Iraqi State Railways in 1947-48. Those that became the Iraqi Class TD operated until the Seventies. One example, No. 1429, was still intact though non-operational in Baghdad, only recently.

The Middle East Forces moved 15 from Iran to Italy during 1944, after the Allied invasion and fall of Mussolini.

After the war they were sold to Ferrovie dello Stato, for which they became FS Class 737 until the early Fifties.

The Middle East Forces loaned some 8Fs to Palestine Railways during 1942, and in 1947 sold it 24. After the Arab-Israeli War of 1948, 23 Stanier 8Fs were taken over by Israel Railways, which ran them until 1958.

Twenty-five new WD Stanier 8Fs were sold to Turkish State Railways in 1941 but seven of these were lost at sea. Two more locomotives were delivered in 1943, making a total of 20. As the TCDD 45151 class, they operated until the Eighties.

Those 8Fs ordered by the War Department, only for France to capitulate to the Germans sooner than expected, were loaned to British railway companies in 1940, However, in 1941 they were all recalled for military service in Egypt and Iran. The last 24 new WD 8Fs remained in the UK on loan to LMS. The five WD 8Fs, which came back from the Middle East, were in poor condition, and were refurbished for WD use at the Longmoor Military Railway in Hampshire.

Three of these were sold to British Railways in 1957 and became Nos. 48773-75. The other two were transferred to the Cairnryan Military Railway and were scrapped in 1959, bringing to an end the War Department's use of Stanier 8Fs.

A total of 624 Stanier 8Fs were inherited by British Railways in 1948, and as stated above, another 42 were bought from the War Department. They were allocated to the London Midland Region, the successor to the LMS.

Withdrawals by BR began in 1964 and 150 were still running in 1968, the last year of BR steam on the national network.

LMS 8F 2-8-0 No. 8233 hauls a train of military equipment during an open day on the now-closed internal railway at the MoD's Royal Engineers' depot at Long Marston in Warwickshire on October 4, 1987. BRIAN SHARPE

THE SEVERN VALLEY'S GREAT OLD SOLDIER

Fourteen Stanier 8Fs are known to have survived worldwide with six LMS/BR locomotives having been preserved in the UK, while a seventh was used a spares donor for sister locomotives and to supply components for several new-build projects.

One of the saved locomotives may be considered the most widely travelled main line locomotive in the UK heritage fleet, if you exclude LNER A3 Pacific *Flying Scotsman*, which toured North America and Australia in the heritage era.

The Stanier 8F Locomotive Society started as the 8F Preservation Society at the end of British Rail main line steam in 1968, intending to preserve a member of the class and succeeded in saving No. 48773 (LMS No. 8233).

Built in 1940 by North British in Glasgow to serve the War Department, it is among an elite few locomotives that worked on six railways in

three continents; defying the scrap merchants at least six times.

Originally intended to serve in France, when that country fell to the Germans, No. 8233, then WD No. 307, joined sister locomotives on the LMS, spending a year on heavy wartime traffic from Toton, Holbeck and Westhouses depots.

By December 1941, LMS No. 8233 had been requisitioned by the WD and sent to Iran. It became No. 41.109 of the Iranian State Railways and headed supply trains to the USSR.

In 1944, it was converted to oil burning, and two years later was transferred overland to the Suez Canal Zone.

Loaned for two years to the Egyptian State Railways, it returned to the WD's Suez workshops in 1948, needing a new firebox.

Coming within a whisker of being scrapped, it returned to the UK in 1952 for overhaul at Derby Works. Two years later it went to the Longmoor

Military Railway as WD No. 500.

In 1957, it returned to the main line in British Railways' service as No. 48773, based at Polmadie depot in Glasgow. There it was withdrawn twice and reinstated twice.

During the late Sixties, No. 48773 had diagonal yellow stripes painted on the cabsides to indicate that it could not run south of Crewe owing to it being out of gauge for the new 25kV AC overhead electrification. However, as the locomotive's original War Department top-feed had been replaced by one of LMS pattern, it has been argued that the striping was unnecessary since it would have been within the loading gauge.

Its last shed was Rose Grove in 1968, two years after receiving a heavy intermediate repair and overhauled boiler at Crewe Works.

Moves to save No. 48773 – which famously struck a camel in the Iranian desert during its

The Severn Valley Railway's first four main line engines lined up at Bridgnorth on April 6, 1969: left to right, Ivatt 2-6-0 No. 46443, Collett 0-6-0 No. 3205, Ivatt 2-6-0 No. 43106 and Stanier 8F No. 48773. DAVID WILLIAMS

This plate dedicating No. 48773 to British servicemen and women was affixed to the locomotive in 1986. DUNCAN HARRIS*

A 'CHURCHILL' COMES HOME

During the heritage era, three members of the class have, over the years, been repatriated to the UK from Turkey. In that country, the 8Fs were known by the local crews as 'Churchills' after the Prime Minister who sent them out during the Second World War.

As the heritage railway movement blossomed, the supply of scrap steam locomotives available to would-be restorers dwindled, and so prospective owners began to look beyond our shores for British types in exile.

In 1989, fellow enthusiast Mike Hoskins told Andrew Goodman, founder of road haulage company Moveright International, an expert in the carriage of locomotives and rolling stock by road, that he had bought a Stanier 8F in Turkey and needed to get it home. The 8F was Turkish State Railways No. 45160 (WD No. 348) which had been exported to Egypt as a kit of parts in 1940.

Built that year by North British and earmarked for use on a new Western Front, after the fall of France it found itself working in Britain as LMS No. 8274 for a few weeks until 1941.

It then became one of a batch of 25 locomotives exported to Turkey via Egypt as a kit of parts, and one of only 18 to arrive, as the remaining seven were lost at sea when the boat carrying them across the Atlantic sank. On arrival at Port Said, the 8F had been taken by land to Sivas in Turkey where it was reassembled.

Mike and Andrew flew to Istanbul, and not only joined a steam railtour as part of the purchase deal, they spent a week in a railwaymen's hostel while arranging for the 8F to be brought to Mersin, the main port in southern Turkey to be loaded on to a ship for the homeward journey.

The 8F was unloaded at Immingham and then taken to the Swanage Railway, its first restoration base.

In Dorset, it ran for a time in Turkish outline and livery but was later rebuilt as a British 8F.

It was later moved to the Gloucestershire Warwickshire Railway to complete an overhaul, and moved again under its own power for the first time at the line's Toddington base on April 21, 2010. It starred in the Cotswold Festival of Steam GWR 175 celebration on May 29-June 6 that year, taking on the identity of scrapped Swindon-built sister No. 8476.

On October 28, 2012, Turkey's ambassador to London, Ahmet Ünal Çeviköz and his wife Emel, enjoyed Sunday lunch on the Gloucestershire Warwickshire Railway's 'Elegant Excursions' dining train, hauled by the repatriated 8F, carrying its number No. 45160.

The ambassador, along with Brian Simpson MEP and his wife Linda, were dining at the invitation of the Churchill 8F group. He highlighted the repatriation of

wartime service – were sparked by enthusiast Bill Murray after his letter to the Northwich Guardian in 1968 was published. In July that year, the Daily Telegraph highlighted the bid to buy No. 48773 for £3000 and nationwide publicity helped raise the amount.

It headed the Locomotive Club of Great Britain's 'Farewell to Steam Special' on August 4, 1968, and afterwards it passed into the ownership of the 8F Society and was delivered in working order to the SVR, diesel hauled via Toton and Tyseley.

At the time, it was considered by preservationists to be in the best all-round condition of the available 8Fs, with just 36,000 miles on the clock since overhaul.

In 1968 it was the subject of a late appeal to purchase it for preservation, and was taken to the Severn Valley Railway for restoration.

It featured in the first weekend of public running of the heritage line, May 23-24, 1970, running packed trains between Bridgnorth and Hampton Loade.

In 1975, it took part in the Shildon cavalcade as part of the 150th anniversary of the Stockton & Darlington Railway.

It has hauled railtours over the national network and made visits to other heritage lines. The only other Stanier 8F to have run on the main line in the heritage era is Crewe-built No. 48151, owned by the West Coast Railway Company and based at Carnforth.

No. 48773 last ran in 2008, and is currently displayed in the Severn Valley's Engine House museum and visitor centre at Highley,

awaiting overhaul.

As it is a locomotive with a unique military provenance, No. 48773 has been dedicated as a memorial to the railwaymen of the Corps of Royal Engineers (Transportation) who lost their lives in the Second World War.

In 1986, a service of dedication was held at Highley on the Severn Valley Railway, led by the Dean of Hereford conducted with full military honours.

In 2002, the society compiled a roll of honour and books of remembrance commemorating 354 known casualties. The Chief Royal Engineer, Lt-General Sir Scott Grant KCB, dedicated it at a service held at Kidderminster Town station.

Recently the names of a further 54 Second World War casualties have been identified and an additional roll of honour was produced by the society. Brigadier Mike Stephens unveiled it at a ceremony at the Engine House in 2011, together with a roll of honour commemorating the six railway sappers killed in an accident on the Longmoor Military Railway in 1956.

Visitors can see the rolls of honour and information panels describing the history of the railway's Royal Engineers alongside the locomotive.

In 2014, during a routine review of locomotive mileages at the Severn Valley, it was found that No. 48773 topped the mileage charters of the line, in records dating back to 1968.

The 8F had managed to clock up 151,805 miles during the heritage era.

Stanier 8F No. 48773 is displayed inside the Severn Valley Railway's Engine House museum and visitor centre at Highley opposite War Department Austerity 2-10-0 No. WD600 *Gordon*, which also worked on the Longmoor Military Railway. In October 2011, the 1940-built 8F, which was ordered from the North British Locomotive Company of Glasgow by the War Department, became the focal point of a service in the Engine House honouring nine people killed during the Battle of Britain when a German bomber attacked the Melbourne Military Railway near Castle Donington in Derbyshire. SVR

Repatriated 8F No. 8274 still in its Turkish form running at Swanage in September 1989. ANDREW PM WRIGHT

Stanier 8F 2-8-0 No. 8274 again carrying its Turkish cabside plates for the ambassador's visit on October 28, 2012. IAN CROWDER

Stanier 8F No. 8274, again carrying its Turkish number 45160, is seen at Cheltenham Racecourse with its restorers, father-and-son team Mike and Kevin Hoskin. IAN CROWDER

Stanier 8F 2-8-0 No. 8274 in its Turkish identity as No. 45160 resting at Winchcombe before departing with the special 'Elegant Excursions" Sunday luncheon service on October 28, 2012. IAN CROWDER

As LMS No. 8274, the repatriated locomotive hauls a Gloucestershire Warwickshire Railway service train on September 29, 2012. IAN CROWDER

the Stanier 8Fs as a great example of co-operation between the two countries.

The train departed from a rain-soaked Winchcombe station bedecked with UK and Turkish flags while the locomotive carried the country's two flags on the bufferbeam, along with the royal headcode, correct as the ambassador was representing his head of state.

The ambassador was clearly delighted at the visit and the chance to ride on the footplate during the journey. He said: "This is one of the rare elements that bring the history of our two countries together. I very much recognise that there are people who enjoy keeping up the experiences and history of our past."

He said that when he was a university student he regularly travelled between Istanbul and Ankara on trains hauled by steam locomotives. "I remember these engines well and this might even have been one of them," he said. "We knew that they were built in Britain and I appreciate that many locomotives and other engineering was exported to Turkey from Britain."

Owned by the Churchill 8F Locomotive Company, No. 8274 has been based on the Great Central Railway (Nottingham) since 2014.

BACK AGAIN FOR ANOTHER TWO

Moveright International returned to Sivas in December 2010 to repatriate two more 8Fs.

Sister TDCC No. 45166 was acquired by the Churchill 8F Locomotive Company.

However, once it was safely back in Britain, the group quickly decided to sell it in order to finance another project... but there were no UK buyers.

An offer from the municipality of Bee'r Sheva in Israel was forthcoming and accepted.

The derelict locomotive was wanted as the principal exhibit in the Bee'r Sheva regional railway heritage centre in its historic Old Town.

It has been cosmetically restored as Israel Railways No. 70414 (originally WD No. 414), in 1958 condition on static display at the old Beersheba station, a declared National Heritage Site.

The locomotive was moved from Barry to Southampton Docks on November 22, 2012 by Moveright International, arriving at Southampton Docks the following morning, and loaded on to shipping trailers later that day. It was subsequently shipped from Southampton to the port of Ashdod by Grimaldi Lines on the Grande Europa.

No. 45170, which was bought privately, was at first displayed at the Locomotion museum in Shildon along with other military exhibits and then moved to the North Norfolk Railway as a long-term project restoration project.

However, owner John Oldcorn then offered it for sale, and as it was built at Glasgow in 1942, the Scottish Railway Preservation Society eagerly bought it, after it launched an appeal to raise the £120,000.

Scotland fared particularly badly when it came to preserving main line locomotives from the country's main line steam fleet, and here was a golden opportunity to acquire a tender locomotive ripe for full restoration.

Built for the Ministry of Supply, it was first loaned to the LMS then sent to Turkey in 1943 as part of the war effort. At the end of the war it became No. 45170 in the Turkish State Railways fleet.

The locomotive is more than 90% complete and well preserved having spent much of its life in an arid climate. Late in its operating life it was subject to a heavy overhaul and is rated a good candidate for restoration to working order, and potentially main line condition.

It is now housed in the Museum of Scottish Railways at the Bo'ness & Kinneil Railway, which is operated by the SRPS.

On February 20, 2016, an open day was held by the SRPS to support its Spirit of Scotland appeal to compete the purchase of No. 45170 and restore it; a task estimated at £250,000.

Guests of honour at the event were the society's president, multi-millionaire enthusiast Sir William McAlpine, accompanied by his wife Lady Judy McAlpine.

In the evening, attendees were treated to a talk given by Andrew Goodman. The Turkish Consulate-General to Scotland, Northern England and Northern Ireland, Semih Lutfu Turgut, attended.

*If you wish to support the SRPS 45170 Appeal, donations can be made online at mydonate. bt.com/events/stanier8f/. Full information can be found at www.srpssteam.com or by emailing 8f.Appeal@srps.org.uk

Repatriated Stanier 8F No. 45170 was displayed outside Glasgow's SECC Hydro in front of the Finnieston Crane landmark on November 13, 2014, en route to its new home at the Bo'ness & Kinneil Railway. HUGH DOUGHERY

Newly reimported but very unrestored Stanier 8F No. 45170 inside the Locomotion museum at Shildon on October 8, 2011. ROBIN JONES

Sir William McAlpine stands in front of No. 45170, with fundraiser Gavin Johnson to his left, alongside SRPS chairman Vic Michel and Tim Lockett; other SRPS members actively involved in raising money. IAN LOTHIAN

Former Turkish State Railways Class 45151 Stanier 8F No. 45166 at Israel's old Beersheba station, after being cosmetically restored as Israel Railways No. 70414 (WD No. 414), in 1958 condition. MCKABY*

No. 8266 (WD. No. 340, Turkish State Railways No. 45168) displayed at Izmit old railway station in Turkey.

AND THERE'S MORE

Several other Second World War Stanier 8Fs survive in the Middle East in varying forms.

North British 1940-built No. 8266, WD No. 340 (Turkish State Railways No. 45168) is on static display at Izmit old railway station in Turkey.

WD No. 335 (Turkish No. 45165), which dates from 1941, is on static display in the country's Çamlık Railway Museum.

North British No. 8279 (WD No. 335, Turkish No. 45165, which was built in 1940)

was last heard of dumped in Sincan, a town near the Turkish capital Ankara.

There is also believed to be a fourth survivor elsewhere in Turkey.

In Baghdad, 1942-built North British No. 8188 (WD No. 547, Iraqi Republic Railways No. 1429) survived both Gulf Wars and was discovered dumped near a railway yard without a tender. It is now said to be in storage pending formal preservation.

Two others are believed to survive in Iraq, but owing to the political situation and

conflict with Islamic State in recent years, enthusiasts have not seen fit to pursue further lines of inquiry on the ground.

Whether any more are returned to Britain remains to be seen.

Two other 8Fs can be visited only if you have diving equipment.

In the early Fifties, Jacques-Yves Cousteau discovered the wreck of the previously mentioned SS *Thistlegorm* after receiving information from local fishermen. He raised several items from the wreck, which lies around 100ft down on the seabed, including a motorcycle, the captain's safe, and the ship's bell.

In the early Nineties, Sharm el-Sheikh began to develop as a diving resort and recreational diving on the *Thistlegorm* started.

The massive explosion that sank the ship blew much of its midship superstructure away, making it very accessible to divers, who can visit it without specialist equipment and training.

The Times named the *Thistlegorm* as one of the top 10 wreck diving sites in the world.

Trucks, motorcycles, Wellington boots, rifles, Westland Lysander wings, Bristol Mercury radial engine exhaust rings and cylinders, Bristol Blenheim bomber tailplanes, Universal Carrier armoured vehicles and RAF trolley accumulators can be seen. Off to the port side of the wreck, level with the blast area can be found one of the 8Fs, which had been stored as deck cargo.

The other locomotive lies off the starboard side level, but the wreck is rapidly disintegrating and rusting.

One Stanier 8F that will not be repatriated is this one of a pair on the SS *Thistlegorm*, which lies 100ft at the bottom of the Red Sea.
KEVIN BOOTH

CHAPTER II

The War Department Austerities

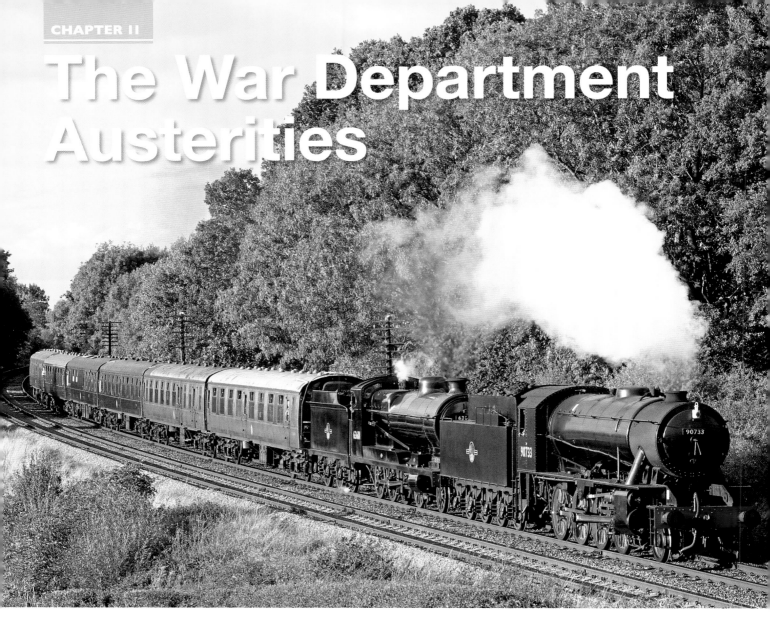

With the outbreak of the Second World War, it became clear that Britain would need an instant but cheaply built generation of locomotives, not only to supplement traffic on the national network, which was now being run by the government again, but for use overseas when the Axis–occupied territories were freed. Cometh the hour, cometh the man – Robert Riddles, best known today for the British Railways Standards.

Robert Riddles based his Austerity 2-8-0 design on the Stanier 8F, which had already been chosen by the government as the standard War Department freight locomotive design for the Second World War.

The director of transportation equipment at the Ministry of Supply (and from 1948 onwards, member of the Railway Executive for Mechanical and Electrical Engineering, the top man in charge of British Railways' locomotive policy), Riddles tweaked and improved the design to apply 'no frills' austerity principles – as with the USATC S160s; a cheaper build but a shorter life expectancy.

His economies included a boiler of simpler construction, which was parallel rather than tapered; and a round-topped firebox rather than a Belpaire one; one made of steel rather than the more expensive copper. The WD 2-8-0 was faster to build with a simple construction using fabricated components instead of heavy expensive castings and cast iron in place of steel for items such as wheel centres.

A total of 935 Austerity 2-8-0s were built between 1943-45, 545 of them by the North British Locomotive Company of Glasgow and 390 by Vulcan Foundry of Newton-le-Willows. Indeed, the first batch of 80 was ordered as LMS 8Fs. Within a few months, they became one of the biggest classes of British steam locomotive of all time.

After D-Day the Army on the continent employed all but three.

Once the conflict was over, the War Department disposed of 930 locomotives, 200 being sold to the LNER where they became Class O7 533s, and more were bought by the British Transport Commission, which set up British Railways in 1948.

In 1946, 12 were exported to Hong Kong, while 184 stayed in service on the continent, most working in The Netherlands for national operator Nederlandse Spoorwegen. One was even exchanged with the USATC for a S160.

The War Department kept two back, and they worked on the Longmoor Military Railway in Hampshire.

On June 2, 1944, WD 2-8-0 No. 7337 was hauling a freight train carrying bombs,

LEFT: One of the locomotive types built for the Second World War doubleheads with the War Department's standard freight engine for the First World War; WD Austerity 2-8-0 No. 90733, built by Vulcan Foundry in 1944 and Great Central Railway 8K (O4) No. 63601, built at Gorton in 1912, at Kinchley Lane on the Great Central Railway. Both engines and the coaches are in later British Railways' livery, although No. 90733, which is based on the Keighley & Worth Valley Railway, was never a BR engine. The pair are seen working together for the first time in preservation on October 4, 2009. DUNCAN HARRIS*

and caught fire as it approached Soham in Cambridgeshire. The train was divided behind the burning wagon, with the front portion being taken forward with the intention of isolating the wagon in open countryside.

The blazing van was close to the station buildings and was obviously liable to endanger life in nearby homes. Driver, Benjamin Gimbert, set the engine in motion and as he approached a signalbox he warned the signalman to stop any trains likely to be involved and indicated what he intended to do.

However, the deadly cargo detonated at the station, killing the LNER fireman, James Nightall, and severely injuring driver Gimbert. Signalman Frank Bridges, who was on the opposite platform, died the next day. For their actions, Gimbert and Nightall were awarded George Crosses for their bravery.

The 733 WD 2-8-0s inherited by British Railways were eventually withdrawn and scrapped, rendering the class extinct.

However, one is still running in Britain today, on the Keighley & Worth Valley Railway.

Built in January 1945 by Vulcan Foundry as works No. 5200, it became WD No. 79257, and was shipped to the continent on completion.

After the war, it was among those sold to the Nederlandse Spoorwegen where it became 4300 class No. 4464.

In 1953 it, along with a sister locomotive, were sold on to Statens Järnvägar, the Swedish State Railways, extensively modified and given the classification G11. At Örebro works it had a new fully enclosed cab and electric lighting and its tender was shortened to enable it to fit Swedish turntables. The chimneys, the originals of which had been replaced with taller ones by the Dutch, were cut down.

Re-emerging in a decidedly Swedish outline and renumbered 1931, it entered service in 1954.

SJ had bought the pair on the cheap, effectively as war surplus, to evaluate if it could replace locomotives obtained through the nationalisation of the private railways during the Forties. However, the trials were less than satisfactory, and with dieselisation looming, no more were bought.

The pair were withdrawn after a few years and stored undercover in an isolated forest clearing in northern Sweden as part of a strategic reserve, after some minor restoration work had been carried out.

KWVR members heard about the survival of WD No. 79257, albeit continental outline, and in September 1972, it was bought by the railway.

It arrived in Hull on January 12, 1973 and was offloaded at Ingrow the following day. The locomotive had clearly been well looked after and needed only a minimal amount of work before it entered traffic on the heritage line, running in its Swedish outline for many years.

It was withdrawn in 1976 and sidelined until 1993 when a heavy overhaul began with the aim of back-converting it to its as-built British guise.

The chassis of an original and historically appropriate eight-wheel tender was bought to replace the Swedish six-wheeler tender and a new one was constructed.

It was decided to continue the series of numbers for repatriated engines on British Railways, and so it became No. 90733, one higher than the last BR WD Austerity 2-8-0, No. 90732 *Vulcan*. Incidentally, WD Stanier 8F No. 48773 was incorrectly given that number when it was taken into BR stock in 1957, after being mistaken for an Austerity 2-8-0.

Once the restoration was complete, No. 90773 returned to Haworth on April 16, 2007 for a period of testing and running-in.

It officially re-entered traffic on Monday, July 23, 2007, and in doing so effectively resurrected a lost class of BR locomotive, plugging a gap in the UK heritage fleet. A 'new build' locomotive at a war surplus price?

BELOW: Heavy freight 2-8-0 No. 90733 with a goods train at Oakworth on the Keighley & Worth Valley Railway. BRIAN SHARPE

BRITAIN'S FIRST 2-10-0S

Riddles based his next type, the WD 2-10-0, on his 2-8-0. The two classes were designed to have interchangeable parts.

The 2-10-0s, which had a parallel boiler and round-topped firebox, had the same power output as the 2-8-0 but a lighter axle load, making them suitable for secondary lines. In the Middle East where there were more railways of lighter construction than in Europe, the 2-8-0s were too heavy with their 16½ ton axle load.

Riddles took the basic WD 2-8-0 layout and extended it with an extra driving wheel set to spread the weight to give an axle loading of just 13½ tons.

While the 2-8-0 had a narrow firebox, the 2-10-0 had a wide firebox placed above the driving wheels, an arrangement common in the USA but unusual in Britain. In the UK, wide fireboxes were normally used only where there was a trailing axle, as with Pacifics.

Riddles's 2-10-0s were the first type with this wheel arrangement to run in Britain, and the country's first major class of 10-coupled engines. In this respect and more, they paved the way for Riddles' BR Standard Fs, which many have argued were the finest steam locomotives produced in Britain. They also have a wide firebox placed above the driving wheels. A distinctive feature of the class is that the middle driving wheels of the class have no flange, to ease turning on tighter tracks.

The WD 2-10-0s were built by North British in two batches. The first 100 appeared in 1943-44 and a second, comprising 50 locomotives, in 1945.

The 2-10-0s were run in on the UK network, and 20 of the first batch went to the Middle East, and most went with the Army to France after D-Day.

Again, The Netherlands was a big customer of war surplus WD locomotives, with Nederlandse Spoorwegen taking 103. They formed the NS

A manufacturer's photograph of WD 2-10-0 No. 3650. THE RAILWAY MAGAZINE

Walsall station in January 1972, with Ivatt 2-6-0 No. 43106 and WD 2-10-0 No. 600 *Gordon* on their way to the Severn Valley Railway. SVR ARCHIVES

WD 2-10-0 No. 600 *Gordon* is one of the star exhibits inside the Engine House museum and visitor centre at Highley on the Severn Valley Railway. ROBIN JONES

WD 2-10-0 No. 600 *Gordon* at Shildon during the Rail 150 Stockton & Darlington anniversary celebrations on August 31, 1975. BRIAN SHARPE

A GOOD HOME FOR *GORDON*

Two remained in WD service at the Longmoor Military Railway in Hampshire, a line that had been built by the Royal Engineers from 1903 in order to train soldiers on railway construction and operations.

The line was closed on October 31, 1969, because of the reducing role of the military in an increasingly smaller British Empire, it was decided by the Ministry of Defence to close the railway.

In the 1952 WD renumbering scheme, the last two WD 2-10-0s Nos. 73651 and 73797, were renumbered and named 600 *Gordon* and 601 *Kitchener* respectively.

Kitchener was later withdrawn and scrapped in 1967, but *Gordon*, which had been named in honour of the Royal Engineers' most famous general, Charles Gordon ('Gordon of Khartoum'), had a very bright future in store.

WD 2-10-0 No. 73798 *North British* stands at Motherwell Depot in 1948. BEN BROOKSBANK

Series 5000II, and had a short working life, with the last being withdrawn in 1952.

Twenty-five were taken into British Railways' ownership. In the main, the Scottish Region operated them on heavy freights and all were withdrawn between 1961-62.

Sixteen went to Greece's Hellenic State Railways and four ended up on the Chemins de Fer Syriens in Syria.

A WD Austerity 2-10-0 at work in Scotland in 1944. THE RAILWAY MAGAZINE

WD austerity 2-10-0 No. 600 *Gordon* crosses the Victoria Bridge over the River Severn on the Severn Valley Railway. BRIAN SHARPE

The last steam locomotive owned by the British Army, it featured in public steam events at Longmoor, the last being on July 5, 1969.

It also hauled at least one enthusiast tour, along the main line from Woking to Longmoor.

However, when a bid to preserve part of the Longmoor Military Railway failed in the early Seventies, the Transport Trust was asked by the Army to find it a suitable home.

It duly arrived on the Severn Valley Railway in 1972 and entered traffic from July 29 that year. At the time, it was the biggest locomotive to have run on the heritage line.

Fully restored at Bridgnorth Works, in May 1980 it took part in the Locomotive Parade at Rocket 150, the 150th anniversary of the opening of the Liverpool and Manchester Railway at Rainhill.

A very popular performer on the

Severn Valley, *Gordon* has also served as Gordon the Big Engine during the SVR's Day Out With Thomas events.

On July 25, 2008, Gordon was formally handed over by the Army to the Severn Valley, which had been looking after it in a caretaker capacity offically.

At the time of writing, it is awaiting overhaul, and is displayed in the line's Engine House museum at Highley.

TWO WDs FOR THE SUNNY SOUTH

Encouraged by Mid Hants Railway director Ken Woodroofe, in 1984, the line's locomotive superintendent, John Bunch, led a group of locomotive engineers to Greece to inspect out-of-service engines previously provided to the Greek national railway in the aftermath of the Second World War.

"We were fanatical preservationists at that time," John said. "The big attraction was the fact that most of the engines were complete."

After the end of the war, the newly formed United Nations focused on the needs of war-ravaged countries and finding means of supplying urgently required materials. In Greece, which has just 94 standard gauge engines, only 46 were worth repairing.

In October 1945 the British military authorities in Egypt declared that the 16 WD 2-10-0s in store there were surplus to requirements, and so they were all sent to Greece where they became Class Lb.

In Greece, they were converted to right-hand drive and fitted with headlamps with a second roof with the chimneys lengthened and a small deflector fitted behind them.

They were allocated to the Thessalonica Division in the northern part of the country and divided up between the depots at Thessalonica, Drama, Alexandroupolis and Pithion (Pythio). During the Sixties they were in regular use, hauling the Istanbul express between Thessalonica and Pithion as well as the Athens to Yugoslavia International express between Thessalonica and the border.

WD Austerity 2-10-0 No. 90775, then painted as Longmoor Military Railway No. 601 *Sturdee*, climbs Medstead bank on the Mid Hants Railway on April 10, 1988. BRIAN SHARPE

However, by 1967 dieselisation was underway in the Thessalonica Division so the 2-10-0s were then concentrated in the eastern part where some lines required locomotives with a light axle load. The last 2-10-0 was withdrawn in 1979.

The visit by John Bunch's party proved successful. Two engines, WD 2-10-0 No. 951 and a USATC S160 2-8-0, were brought back to Ropley Works for overhaul. A second WD 2-10-0, the former No. WD73672, was also bought and initially went to the Lavender Line in Sussex.

Before they left Greece, many worn parts had been interchanged with better ones from redundant sisters, and a large number of 'new' spare parts including some complete fireboxes still in their North British crates were obtained.

No. 951, which arrived in the UK at Ipswich Docks in August 1984 on board the Greek vessel *Empress*, was bought by John Bunch and Harvey Katz and given the fictitious BR number 90775, following on from the original BR number series for repatriated engines, entering traffic in 1988.

As with the 2-8-0 repatriated from Sweden, No. 90775 was stripped of the many foreign fittings that it had gathered during 40 years overseas and returned to an Anglicised appearance. It first appeared on the Mid Hants Railway as No. 90775, but in 1989 it was repainted into Longmoor Military Railway blue and red livery as No. WD601 *Sturdee*.

In 1992, its owners sold it to the Essex Locomotive Society, which transferred it to the North Yorkshire Moors Railway.

However, it soon needed major boiler work and following repairs it was returned to traffic in October 1994 when it was again painted in BR black as No. 90775, but this time with 'British Railways' in full on the tender side.

Around that time, it starred in two episodes of series five of ITV's popular Sixties police drama Heartbeat.

After a further overhaul it left the NYMR in 2002 and moved for a year to the Great Central Railway at Loughborough.

In late June 2003, it moved to the North Norfolk Railway on loan and in the following year was offered for sale for a six-figure sum. With the help of a wealthy supporter, the Midland & Great Northern Joint Railway Society bought it for future use on the NNR, where it remains today.

In BR black, WD 2-10-0 No. 90775 leaves Weybourne for Holt on the North Norfolk Railway in wintry conditions. BRIAN SHARPE

RECOMMISSIONED BY THE FORCES SWEETHEART

On the Lavender Line, No. WD73672 was renumbered No. 3672 and, in honour of the 'forces sweetheart', named *Dame Vera Lynn*, being commissioned on August 6, 1985 by the Dame herself.

Eventually, *Dame Vera Lynn* also moved to the NYMR and entered traffic in 1989. Over the next decade it clocked up more than 100,000 miles in traffic, and was a hugely popular performer.

However, its boiler ticket ran out in October 1998, leaving it to await its place in the overhaul queue.

In 2014, a £750,000 nationwide appeal was launched to pay for its overhaul under the banner of the Fight for Vera Fund, with the aim of having it back in steam by 2019, its 75th anniversary.

The Fight for Vera Fund would also like to see the locomotive become a national memorial to the people who built it during a time of international hardship.

A third WD Austerity 2-10-0 is preserved at the Nederlands Spoorwegmuseum (Dutch Railway Museum) in Utrecht.

Built by North British in 1945 as works No. 25601, No. WD 73755 has been named *Longmoor* in honour of the former military railway.

It was the 1000th British-built freight locomotive to be shipped to the continent since D-Day.

After the war, it was one of the WD locomotives sold to Nederlandse Spoorwegen and became No. 50785.

It was withdrawn in 1952 and set aside for preservation.

3672 *Dame Vera Lynn*

NEEDS YOU
Please text DAME13 to 70070 to donate £10.00

WD Austerity 2-10-0 No. 3672 *Dame Vera Lynn* passes Green End on the North Yorkshire Moors Railway on May 27, 1996. DAVID IDLE/NYMR

TOP LEFT: WD 2-10-0 No. 3672 *Dame Vera Lynn* departs from Goathland en route to Pickering on the North Yorkshire Moors Railway on October 26, 1989. BRIAN SHARPE

WD Austerity 2-10-0 *Dame Vera Lynn* when it first arrived on the Lavender Line.

No. WD 73755 *Longmoor* inside the Nederlands Spoorwegmuseum (Dutch Railway Museum). Since 1954 the engine has been housed in the 1874-built Maliebaan station on the Eastern Railway in Utrecht.

The splendid standard wartime shunter

One of the most successful steam engine designs ever to run in Britain, and certainly one of the simplest is the Austerity 0-6-0ST. It was designed by the Hunslet Engine Company for the Ministry of Supply for use as the standard Second World War shunting engine, and has been the mainstay of services on many heritage lines at some stage in their history. 56 of them survived for preservation purposes, many providing motive power on heritage lines today.

Robert Stephenson & Hawthorn's 0-6-0ST No. 71515 *Mech Navvies Ltd* heads the Pontypool & Blaenavon Railway's vintage train from Blaenavon. ALISTAIR GRIEVE

The Keighley & Worth Valley Railway acquired Hunslet No. 3791 of 1953 WD191 straight from Army service, following its withdrawal on the Longmoor Military Railway in 1968. It arrived at Tenterden in February 1972. It is seen heading a service train to Tenterden in August 2014. ROBIN JONES

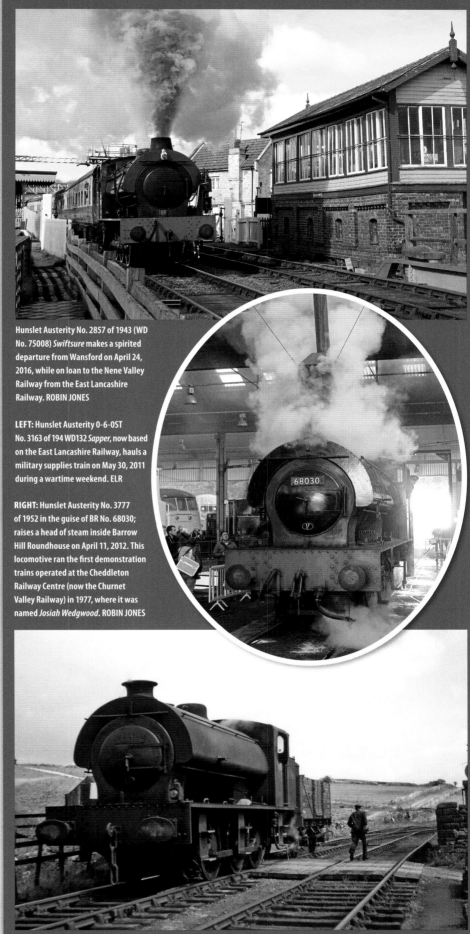

At the outbreak of the Second World War, the War Department chose the LMS 3F 'Jinty' 0-6-0T as its standard shunting locomotive. However, Leeds manufacturer Hunslet successfully argued that a simplified version of its more modern 50550 design would be more suitable.

These engines have a history quite different to that of any other type of engine. In fact they had a life expectancy of only two years, yet some have now been promoted to front-line passenger service after 40 years of hard work.

The inside-cylinder 0-6-0ST was manufactured by a number of locomotive builders before the war for industrial service and the various designs continually evolved, with little standardisation.

Hunslet had a standard design for many years, which had 16in diameter cylinders, a round saddle tank not covering the smokebox, and a sloping coal bunker.

The next logical development was to increase cylinder diameter to 18in for more power, and extend the tank over the smokebox, for greater water capacity.

The company's 48150 class was built for the Guest Keen Baldwins Iron & Steel Company in 1937, being an enlarged version of a design dating from 1923.

These were developed in 1941-42, with various modifications, and the 18in saddle tank was born, which Hunslet called the

Hunslet Austerity No. 2857 of 1943 (WD No. 75008) *Swiftsure* makes a spirited departure from Wansford on April 24, 2016, while on loan to the Nene Valley Railway from the East Lancashire Railway. ROBIN JONES

LEFT: Hunslet Austerity 0-6-0ST No. 3163 of 194 WD132 *Sapper*, now based on the East Lancashire Railway, hauls a military supplies train on May 30, 2011 during a wartime weekend. ELR

RIGHT: Hunslet Austerity No. 3777 of 1952 in the guise of BR No. 68030; raises a head of steam inside Barrow Hill Roundhouse on April 11, 2012. This locomotive ran the first demonstration trains operated at the Cheddleton Railway Centre (now the Churnet Valley Railway) in 1977, where it was named *Josiah Wedgwood*. ROBIN JONES

The real J94 No. 68013 – as opposed to the Austerity 0-6-0STs that have taken that number in preservation. Pictured at Middleton Top on the legendary Cromford & High Peak line in July 1959, it was outshopped by Hunslet on June 30, 1944, became WD No. 75125, and was transferred to the LNER in June 1946, when it became No. 8013. Shedded at Immingham at Nationalisation, it was withdrawn from Derby shed on August 31, 1964, and scrapped by Cashmores of Great Bridge that November. COLOUR RAIL

Hunslet Austerity No. 66 – the last standard gauge steam locomotive built in Britain for use in Britain – returned to traffic at Buckinghamshire Railway Centre at midday on May 3, 2015 for the first time in 45 years after a nine-year overhaul. GEOFF COURTNEY

Andrew Goodman's Barclay Austerity 0-6-0ST Wemyss Private Railway No. 15 *Earl David* (No. 2183 of 1943, WD No. 71529) in its two-tone lined brown livery, was used on the special train to open the Nene Valley Railway's new Yarwell station on April 4, 2008. ROBIN JONES

Hudswell Clarke Austerity No. 1782 of 1945, which became War Department No. 71505 (WD118) and later Longmoor Military Railway No. 118 *Brussels*, on display inside the Keighley & Worth Valley Railway's Oxenhope museum. ROBIN JONES

'50550' class. It looked much like what became the Austerity, but still had a sloping coal bunker, smaller wheels and sometimes a deeper bufferbeam. Only eight of the 50550s were built, and remarkably, three survive in preservation.

The Hunslet 18in saddle tank, with some modifications, was adopted as standard shunting power, and Robert Riddles, director of transportation equipment at the Ministry of Supply made a very brave decision in opting for a relatively untried design. Extra locomotives for the war effort were needed fast, and in large quantities: there would be no room for unsuccessful designs that couldn't deliver the goods.

Britain's independent locomotive builders were given the job of turning out saddle tanks instead of tanks as quickly as possible. Hunslet subcontracted some of the construction to Barclay, William Bagnall, Hudswell Clarke, Robert Stephenson & Hawthorns and Vulcan Foundry in order to meet delivery requirements.

Production continued long after the war, as the design was so successful. The number of Austerity 0-6-0STs eventually totalled 485 by 1964, of which Hunslet built 217.

They shunted at Army ordnance depots all over Britain and Europe, and when the war ended, many continued in Ministry of Defence service for many years. Production was still in full swing at the end of the war, with huge volumes of traffic still to be shifted, and the Army continued to take delivery of large numbers of engines, although some went straight into store.

The LNER bought 75 of the stored examples and classified them J94, the prefix 'J' referring to an 0-6-0. This description stuck, and many a saddle tank of this design is often erroneously referred to as a J94. Ninety were kept by the military for use on their railways. A further 14 were ordered in 1952 by the Army to supplement its 90 existing engines.

The engines entered LNER service in Army khaki livery but with their LNER numbers in the series 8006 to 8080, and many were not painted black until BR days when they acquired the numbers 68006 to 68080.

After D-Day they were well-dispersed across Europe, North Africa and the Middle East, and many found themselves in main line or industrial service overseas, when they were 'demobbed' after the war, though it is not generally known that many of those

travelling abroad with the Army, didn't actually do anything.

Twenty-seven that had been loaned to Nederlandse Spoorwegen were sold to that company in 1947, becoming the NS 8800 class. A further 11 were loaned to the Nederlandsche Staatsmijnen, which bought nine.

Others were sold for industrial use. As the final War Department locomotives were being delivered, the National Coal Board was placing orders for identical locomotives to be used at its collieries. Between 1948 and 1964, 77 new Austerity 0-6-0STs were built for the NCB.

The Yorkshire Engine Company also built eight locomotives to this design in 1954 for use in ironstone quarries and at Scunthorpe Steelworks. Hunslet undertook the rebuilding of many NCB locomotives and when the Army started to sell off locomotives again in 1959, the Leeds manufacturer bought 15 examples that were to be rebuilt and sold on. The NCB bought 13 of these, the 14th was sold directly into preservation and the final locomotive was scrapped without being rebuilt. The rebuilds had underfeed stokers but these were not a great success in the long run.

Hunslet No. 3798 of 1953 WD198 *Royal Engineer* in Havenstreet yard on its Isle of Wight Steam Railway home on August 7, 2006. It moved to the island on loan from the National Army Museum in 1991 and ownership was transferred to the heritage line in 2008. HEC TATE*

Hunslet No. 2855 of 1943 is the oldest of the surviving Hunslet Austerity 0-6-0STs. Renamed War Department No. 75006 after the war it went to the National Coal Board (Opencast Executive) at Llanharan Disposal Point as No. L1, following which it was later transferred to NCB-OE Onllwyn, where it is pictured on New Year's Day, 1969. It is now based at the Nene Valley Railway, where it has carried the mock BR number 68081. HUGH LLEWELLYN*

Longmoor Military Railway blue-liveried Hunslet Austerity 0-6-0ST No. 3792 of 1953 W192 *Waggoner* passes the Isle of Wight Steam Railway's award-winning Train Story visitor centre while departing from Havenstreet. The engine moved to the island on loan from the National Army Museum in 2005 and ownership was transferred to the railway in 2008. IOWSR

In BR black livery and carrying the mock BR number 68013, *Royal Pioneer* is seen in Peak Rail service in 2012. Built by Robert Stephenson & Hawthorns as No. 7136 of 1944, it became War Department No. 75186, and was the last of the type to be rebuilt by Hunslet, in 1969, when it became No. 3892. It has run in preservation as *Warrington* and WD150. Many heritage lines relied on industrial saddle tanks for their initial operations, and several repainted Austerity 0-6-0STs into BR liveries with fictitious numbers as an easy way of getting a 'main line' locomotive 'on the cheap'. ROB BENDALL*

Hunslet No. 2868 was one of the engines sold by the MoD back to Hunslet for rebuilding. In 1961, it emerged from works with a new number, 3883, and was loaned to BR Western Region, which used it as shed pilot at Swindon.

The NCB continued to use Austerity 0-6-0STs into the early Seventies and a small number remained in service until the early Eighties, notably at Bickershaw Colliery in Greater Manchester.

It also worked main line trains of 38 empty vans plus a GWR dynamometer car at Kingham in April 1963; this was the last occasion when a dynamometer car was used in Britain for scientific research on steam traction. The engine was resold to the NCB, which used it at the Glasshoughton coking plant near Castleford. It is now privately owned, named *Lord Phil*, and based at Peak Rail.

Overall, the BR J94s led a quiet life, mainly in the North-East, and enthusiasts paid them little attention. Perhaps their only moment of glory was when Nos. 68006 and 68012 found themselves taking over part of the Cromford & High Peak line for its last few years. They even worked brakevan tours carrying passengers to mark the line's closure, probably the only time a J94 ever hauled a passenger train before the heritage era. These two last surviving 'real' J94s were scrapped.

The class was withdrawn relatively early by BR as 350hp diesel shunters became the first success story of the modernisation programme.

The last new Hunslet Austerity, No. 3890, was built in February 1964 for the NCB, and is of paramount historical importance, as it was the last standard gauge steam locomotive built in this country for non-heritage use in Britain. It marked the end of a 160-year era, during which British steam locomotive manufacturers had become

recognised and respected throughout the world as railways transformed the lives of millions of people.

It arrived at Cadeby Main Colliery at Conisbrough, near Doncaster, the following month, carrying number 66. In 1970 the area was designated a smokeless zone and the 0-6-0ST was stored out of use after a service life of just six years.

A few years after being taken out of use No. 66 was put up for sale, and a member of the Quainton Railway Society outbid 20 rivals – including the National Railway Museum – to become its new owner. The 0-6-0ST arrived at the society's Buckinghamshire Railway Centre base at Quainton Road near Aylesbury in November 1975, and joined the restoration queue, with the main problem being worn tyres owing to it having operated at the colliery over severe gradients and track six inches deep in slurry.

Eventually, in 2006, the £140,000 overhaul started, with the chassis, tyres, boiler and springs being sent to outside contractors but the other work handled in-house by the 'Team 66' group of volunteers. And on May 3, 2015 came their day of well-earned glory, when the No. 66, now fully restored and looking resplendent in NCB green, came off shed to re-enter service after 45 years.

The last Austerity 0-6-0ST rebuild was that of No. 7136 of 1944, which was completed in 1969 when it was renumbered 3892. It was never sold back into industry, and instead went straight into preservation at the now-closed Dinting Railway Centre. It is now based at Peak Rail, and carries the name *Royal Pioneer*.

When built the Austerity 0-6-0STs had a life expectancy of two years. However, more than seven decades after the war ended, many are still giving sterling service on our heritage railways.

In early 2016, Hunslet Austerity 0-6-0ST No. WD196 *Errol Lonsdale* became the first of its class to steam in Belgium in nearly 70 years, in readiness for its guest appearance at the spring Maldegem Steam Festival. Built for the War Department as No. 3796 of 1953, it spent much of its working life on the Longmoor Military Railway in Hampshire in blue livery, up to the line's closure. While on the LMR, an early preservation venue, No. WD196 gained stardom in the film The Great St Trinian's Train Robbery, appearing with George Cole and a number of St Trinian's pupils on the footplate! Originally bought for preservation on the Mid Hants Railway, there it was named *Errol Lonsdale* in March 1978 by Maj Gen Errol Lonsdale, Col Commandant of the Royal Corps of Transport from 1969-74. Arriving on the South Devon Railway early in the days of operation by the South Devon Railway Trust following the end of the Dart Valley Railway era when steam locomotives were in short supply, *Errol Lonsdale* was soon hauling even the heaviest trains. It was repainted from LMR blue livery and given BR black livery and the mock number 68011, in sequence to those carried by Austerities, which were taken into LNER and later BR stock. *Errol Lonsdale* was sold by the SDR in 2009 and moved to The Netherlands. KEVIN HOGGETT

Don't

Each September, North Norfolk undergoes an invasion. In 2015, police estimated than more than 50,000 visitors arrived in Sheringham for the North Norfolk Railway's annual Forties weekend.

tell him, Pike!

Many of the visitors come suitably attired, and do not look out of place with the army of re-enactors who take part in what is one of the biggest events of its kind in Britain.

The event today is far bigger than just the railway, for the whole town and other places along the line join in, with shops, pubs and cafes transformed back to the Forties. Shop window displays are dressed in the style of the era and eateries serve Forties cuisine.

There's music, dancing, food and drink from the NAAFI, memorabilia stalls offer vintage clothing galore, and mini museums of a bygone age on railways and the home front. Military vehicles, an Anderson shelter, homemade jams and pickles, fruit and vegetables are on offer, as well as vintage busses running between stations, a vintage car display at the line's terminus of Holt and also aircraft displays.

North Norfolk Railway general manager, Trevor Eady, says: "It's growing and has the potential to be even bigger."

Adding: "The one thing that is obvious is that you can become part of the event, just by digging some clothes out of your cupboard you are part of it.

"You are integral rather than just turning up in your jeans and T-shirt."

In 2015, 12,000 travelled on the railway during the event, which has extended the resort's summer season and boosted the locality's tourist trade and economy.

The 2016 event, to be held on September 17-18, will be the railway's 24th.

However, go back in time to before when the Forties weekends began, and on the same railways you would – maybe for a few days only – have found some of the greatest Second World War re-enactors of them all.

The Walmington-on-Sea Home Guard platoon stand to attention as what they thought was the Royal Train arrives at the town station (Weybourne) during the filming of an episode for BBC TV's Dad's Army in May 1973. GD KING

THE ROYAL TRAIN

Dad's Army was – and still is a much-loved BBC sitcom, written by Jimmy Perry and David Croft – which ran from 1968 to 1977. It featured the Second World War exploits of the Walmington-on-Sea Home Guard led by the pompous Captain Mainwaring and supported by the indecisive but knowledgeable Sergeant Wilson.

The original idea for the series came from Perry's own experiences in the Local Defence Volunteers (LDV) or Home Guard as it was later called. Perry was only 15 when he joined the Hertfordshire Battalion and Private Pike and Mavis Pike are clearly based on himself and his mother. While serving in the platoon he also came across a veteran of Kitchener's campaigns who used to talk about the 'Fuzzy Wuzzies' – which provided the inspiration for Corporal Jones.

The TV show ran for nine series and 80 episodes in total, plus a radio version based on the television scripts, a 2016 feature film and a stage show. It regularly gained audiences of 18 million viewers and is still repeated worldwide.

The Home Guard consisted of local volunteers otherwise ineligible for military service, either because of age (hence the nickname 'Dad's Army') or by being in professions exempt from conscription.

Dad's Army was voted fourth in a BBC poll to find Britain's Best Sitcom. Radio Times magazine listed Captain Mainwaring's "You stupid boy!" among the 25 greatest put-downs on TV.

Who can forget the inimitable characters played by Clive Dunn, Arthur Lowe, John Laurie, John Le Mesurier, James Beck, Ian Lavender, Arnold Ridley, Frank Williams, Edward Sinclair and Bill Pertwee?

The show made household names of these main characters: indeed, many of their lines and catchphrases have passed into legend – "They don't like it up 'em", "We're doomed!" "Put that light out," "Don't' panic!" Most immortalised of all is the line when a captured U-boat captain asks Pike for his name after he sings a school playground song insulting Hitler and Captain Mainwaring orders, "Don't tell him Pike!"

The series derived much humour from the fact that all the leading characters had 'day jobs' in Walmington-on-Sea. Mainwaring, Wilson and Pike all worked in Swallow Bank, while Jones was the butcher, ARP warden Hodges the greengrocer, Frazer the undertaker and Walker the local spiv and black marketeer. Part of the artistic brilliance of the series was the fact that the characters were all stereotypes of everyday people who you would meet in the Forties.

Each episode saw the platoon trying to protect England from Nazi invasion, with bumbling degrees of success.

Walmington-on-Sea was a fictional town on the south coast, like Romney Marsh at the forefront of the invasion threat.

However, much of the location filming was undertaken in and around Thetford – including the Stanford training area – in the landlocked heart of Norfolk, a world away from the white cliffs of Dover or Beachy Head. Many local residents from the surrounding countryside appeared as extras.

The third episode of the sixth TV series was filmed on the North Norfolk Railway in May 1973, and transmitted on November

14 that year. In the episode, Mainwaring's platoon is assigned to form the guard of honour when King George VI passes through Walmington by train.

A train arrives, but it is the wrong one, a local service pulling only one coach, and its driver and fireman both fall asleep after drinking tea accidentally sweetened with Mrs Mainwaring's sleeping pills. Now the platoon must move the train to clear the line for the King's train.

Mummy's boy Pike tells Mainwaring he can drive the train, so while the stationmaster is on the telephone, the platoon climbs on to the footplate and sets off. However, the stationmaster rushes out after they have gone, clutching the steam brake wheel.

Sentry duty outside the signalbox. NNR

The night watch on the road to Paris. NNR

A display of Second World War Jeeps during the wartime weekend. NNR

Hudswell Clarke 0-6-0ST No. 1700 of 1938 Wissington, a veteran of Norfolk's Wissington Light Railway, stands by at Sheringham station during the Forties weekend. NNR

Waiting for the next train back to base. NNR

"Wot's all this then?" a Forties policeman tackles a miscreant – no Taser here, but a good old-fashioned truncheon. The British Railways sign in the background is a few years premature. NNR

Ladies' fashion of the day on parade in Sheringham. NNR

The Forties clothes stall. NNR

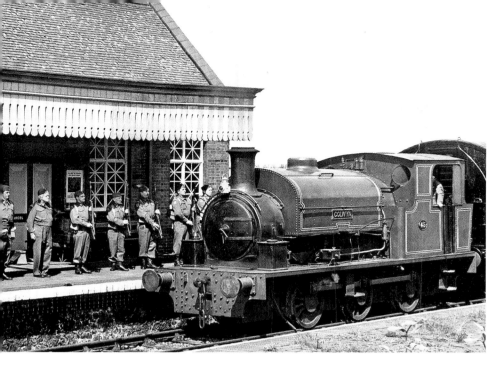

Northamptonshire ironstone quarries and mines internal system.

In the early days of operational standard gauge preservation, industrial saddle tanks often formed the mainstay of services on nascent heritage lines. They were bought out of industry in working order having been regularly maintained, whereas a main line type authentic to a particular railway would probably need extensive and expensive restoration over several years. Needs must – at least you were delivering a steam train to the fare-paying public.

The use of the railway for filming Dad's Army was a major feather in the cap for the volunteers working to restore it.

The North Norfolk Railway had its origins in an overly ambitious scheme to save the entire Midland & Great Northern joint Railway system when it closed in 1959. Eventually, the saviours edited their dreams to just taking over the most scenic section of all, after the briefly surviving Sheringham to Melton Constable stub lost its services in 1964.

The operating company, North Norfolk Railway plc, was launched in 1965 following the granting of two Light Railway Orders. It was later extended to a new station at Kelling Heath, named Holt, half a mile away from the town where the original station lay. Also, in 2010, largely as a result of a drive by the line's chairman, Julian Birley, it was reconnected to the Network Rail main line at Sheringham by the reinstatement of the Station Road level crossing.

In the cab, Pike tells Mainwaring that he can't stop the train, starting a panic among the men. Frazer spots that the vicar, verger, warden and Mayor are chasing them on a hand-powered truck.

Mainwaring starts to make his way over the top of the train to retrieve the brake wheel that air raid warden Hodges is brandishing, and has to save Jones from falling off several times.

Once they reach the back of the train, Hodges throws the wheel, and Mainwaring catches it, then starts to make his way back to the cab. While he and Jones are on top of the train, Pike sends the engine into reverse to stop it, and they are nearly thrown off.

Eventually, they manage to return the train to Walmington (Weybourne) station, just in time to hear the real Royal Train approaching. The platoon must parade just where they are by the line, as they do not have enough time to run back on to the platform.

However, they are standing in front of a water trough, so when the train goes past they all get soaked.

The clip of the Royal Train used in the episode is that of of a Gresley streamlined A4 Pacific on the East Coast Main Line near Burnmouth in the Scottish Borders.

The locomotive heading the local train would never have been used on a main line passenger train. It was Kitson 0-6-0ST No. 5470 of 1933 *Colwyn*, No. 45 in the Stewarts & Lloyds fleet on the

Red lipstick was the fashion in those days! NNR

A US military photographer prepares to join the linesiders. NNR

Female military personnel on duty at Weybourne. NNR

A Forties couple stroll past a station heavily defended by sandbags. NNR

This statue, by Sean Hedges-Quinn, is situated close to the centre of Thetford, the filming location for much of the Dad's Army TV series, which ran from 1968-77. Actors and crew stayed at the nearby Bell and Anchor hotels. PETER TRIMMING*

An engine driver buys his newspaper from a platform vendor.

LNER B12 4-6-0 No. 8572 coupled to a rake of matching teak coaches creates a perfect Forties scene as it approaches Weybourne en route from Sheringham. OWEN BUSHELL/NNR

The Walmington-on-Sea post office inside the Bressingham museum next to the branch of Swallow Bank where George Mainwaring was manager. BSM

Corporal Jack Jones' butchers shop at Bressingham. BSM

The North Norfolk Railway is not the only heritage line in a county that is also home to the Mid-Norfolk Railway and Bure Valley Railway, not to mention Bressingham Steam Museum near Diss.

The late internationally renowned horticulturist and steam aficionado Alan Bloom MBE established the 220-acre gardens at Bressingham Hall, which he bought in 1946, after selling his previous 36-acre site at Oakington in Cambridgeshire.

In the Sixties, responding to the demise of steam, Alan began to collect redundant railway engines as well as steam road and agricultural vehicles, to form the basis of a museum. He gave a welcome bolthole to BR Britannia Pacific No. 70013 *Oliver Cromwell* after it was withdrawn in 1968. The museum has several narrow gauge lines and a standard gauge demonstration line.

Since 2000, Bressingham has been the official home to the Dad's Army Appreciation Society's collection of vehicles and artefacts.

A special indoor exhibition comprises a re-creation of Walmington on Sea.

Jones' butchers shop and the church hall where the platoon held their parades, Frazer's Funeral Parlour and the Swallow Bank can be seen.

Bressingham was happy to lend to the BBC some of its historic collection to feature in the TV show, including traction engine *Bertha*, road roller *Boxer* and the Leyland fire engine, which appeared in episode 50, Brain versus Brawn, in 1972.

Bressingham has been the official home of the Dad's Army Appreciation Society's collection since 2000.

The exhibition comprises a re-creation of Walmington-on-Sea the fictional home to Captain Mainwaring and his men.

This Leyland fire engine starred in an episode of Dad's Army filmed at Santon Downham and Walnut Tree Farm, Bressingham in 1972. BSM

Steam traction and road engines that featured in the TV series. BSM

The room in the church hall, which was used as Captain Mainwaring's office. BSM

DAD'S ARMY: THE SECOND COMING

In 2015, the North Yorkshire Moors Railway entered the Day's Army camp.

It and several other locations in North Yorkshire were selected for the location filming of a new big-screen version, 38 years after the last episode of the original had been transmitted.

Many have long considered that a Dad's Army remake was the one that couldn't be done. How on earth can you reasonably expect to replicate the immortal characters as brilliantly created by the original cast? Or should you simply switch the action to another Home Guard platoon in another part of the country?

In recent times, several amateur dramatic societies have performed versions of Dad's Army with varying degrees of success.

However, sceptics did not believe that a new movie version, with new actors playing the old parts, could succeed.

The film is set during 1944, with the end of the Second World War in sight. Captain Mainwaring's Home Guard is suffering from low morale, until a glamorous journalist played by Catherine Zeta-Jones arrives, purportedly to report on the platoon's exploits.

Meanwhile, MI5 has discovered a radio signal transmitted from Walmington-on-Sea towards Berlin, apparently the work of a spy, giving the Home Guard a chance to make a real difference to the outcome of the war.

The film stars Bill Nighy, Toby Jones, Tom Courtenay, Michael Gambon, Blake Harrison, Daniel Mays and Bill Paterson.

Two actors from the TV shows made brief appearances. Ian Lavender, who had played mummy's boy Pike, returned as Brigadier Pritchard, while at the age of 84, Frank Williams, reprised his role as Rev Timothy Farthing – and hardly looked a day older!

The railway's involvement was comparatively small. The opening scenes saw LMS 'Black Five' 4-6-0 No. 45428 heading through a wooded valley on the NYMR, and then there were scenes in which a Nazi spy was chased through a carriage.

Later on, when Sergeant Wilson was wrongly suspected of being a spy, we see him sitting at Pickering station while his Home Guard

LMS 'Black Five' 4-6-0 No. 45428, star of the opening scenes of the 2016 Dad's Army movie, at Moorgates on the North Yorkshire Moors Railway. BRIAN SHARPE

comrades arrest him. You can glimpse LNER teak coaches in the background – would they have been present on the Southern Railway in 1944? Maybe as a through troop train.

Directed by Oliver Parker and written by David Croft with a screenplay by Hamish McColl, the film was released in the UK by Universal Pictures on February 5, 2016.

Critical reception was mixed. Peter Bradshaw in The Guardian wrote: "Do panic: the cast pull off a convincing impression – and Catherine Zeta-Jones adds sauce – but there's something inescapably creaky about this strangest of sitcom revivals."

Robbie Collin of the Daily Telegraph wrote: "The beloved sitcom marches to the big screen armed with feeble gags. But thanks to a game cast – especially Toby Jones's Captain Mainwaring – it's not quite doomed.

"But it often feels like the film is working through a checklist, and there is a grim moment around 20 minutes from the end when you realise the cast is rattling through all the catchphrases they haven't got round to saying yet."

Nick de Semlyen of Empire wrote: "It

has a strong, game cast but this is karaoke filmmaking, trading on nostalgia rather than breaking new territory. Affable but forgettable."

As a big childhood fan of the original series, I went to see the film within days of its release, fearing the worst. In short, I was very impressed and thoroughly enjoyed every twist and turn.

As with tribute bands, you are never going to get the original stars on stage, and you buy your ticket on that understanding. The acid test is how far can they replicate the original sound, bearing in mind they are five goals down before they even kick a ball.

In this respect, the movie succeeded admirably, and while the white chalk cliffs of Flamborough Head are not entirely like those on the south coast, it was by no means the worst afternoon I have spent at a matinee. If anything, it adds to the Dad's Army legend.

If there is to be a follow up, maybe they could restage Hurricane's armoured train on the Romney, Hythe & Dymchurch Railway, which would at least be in the right part of the world for the script.

Until then, Norfolk remains the heartland of Dad's Army culture.

The cast of the 2016 Dad's Army film. UNIVERSAL PICTURES

Captain Mainwaring (Toby Jones) pays wishful attention to journalist Rose Winters (Catherine Zeta-Jones). UNIVERSAL PICTURES

They came in the Atlantic convoys that ran the gauntlet of U-boats, and then they ran over Britain's railways. Suddenly, they were gone – shipped over to liberated Europe following D-Day. Several of the remarkable United States Army Transportation Corps S160 heavy freight 2-8-0s have found their way back to Britain and can be seen in action on heritage lines.

CHEDDLETON STATION

Oversexed, overpaid, oversized and steaming over here!

During the Second World War, a steam locomotive type, the outline of which nobody in Britain had seen the like of before, was steaming over our network, and in the service of the Big Four companies, too.

When the USA entered the conflict, the United States Army Transportation Corps saw the urgent need for a cheap and efficient locomotive type that could be employed on the wrecked railways of Europe, hauling both military hardware and civilian freight.

Major JW Marsh of the US Army Corps of Engineers looked at two earlier designs, one an update of a Baldwin Locomotive Works' First World War design in contingency for war transportation, which became the S159 class. The other was the S200 2-8-2 class, which was introduced in 1941 and Lend-Leased to the UK for use in the Middle East, and fitted into the British loading gauge.

He produced a blueprint for the S160 Consolidation class of 2-8-0, again on austerity principles and with an emphasis on efficient and fast construction speed rather than longevity, and so compromises in design were made.

With cast frames and cast wheels, the front two driving axles were sprung independently from the rear two driving axles to allow for running on poor-quality track. The larger eight-wheel tender layout was derived from the similar design for the British WD Austerity 2-8-0, (which itself was based upon a First World War design for the US Army for use in Europe) with the coal bunker inset above the water tank to improve visibility when running backwards.

Features that were uncommon in Britain at that time, included a large enclosed cab area, an air gap for maintenance purposes between the wheels and the boiler, a sand container on top of the boiler in order that the heat would keep the sand dry, a Westinghouse brake pump by the smokebox door, and, less obvious, the use of bar frames, instead of frames made from solid sheets of steel.

A total of 800 S160s were built in 13 batches in 1942-43 by ALCO, Baldwin and Lima Locomotive Works, and also supplied on a Lend-Lease basis. Incidentally, although S160 has been popularly adopted as the class identification for this type, it has never been verified as an official designation. The Baldwin designation for the design, 2-8-0-19S, is found on some drawings, and is stamped on to major locomotive components on examples built by the firm.

The S160s were shipped to South Wales and despatched from the GWR shed at Newport, Ebbw Junction. No. 1604 attended a handover ceremony at Paddington station on December 11, 1942, when it entered service in Britain. Attached to

Raw power from across the pond: Greg Wilson's S160 No. 6046 in full flight on the Churnet Valley Railway. FRED KERR

the smokebox were the flags of the USA and Britain. During the ceremony Lord Leathers, Minister of War Transport, formally accepted the locomotive from Col NA Ryan, chief of transportation, US Army.

ENTERING UK SERVICE

The first 43 locomotives were transferred to the LNER's works at Doncaster for completion and running in over the East Coast Main Line. Each of the Big Four companies eventually deployed a total of 400 S160s for 'running-in' purposes while they awaited shipping to the continent for D-Day. In reality, rather than being tested, they were replacing damaged stock and increasing the capacity of the British network to facilitate the movement of military equipment and troops. From the

Celebrated as liberation locomotives by the French, a US servicewoman cracks a bottle of Champagne over the cylinders of newly delivered S160 at Cherbourg on January 23, 1945. Its purpose is to head fast freights from the port to Paris. US NATIONAL ARCHIVES

S160 2-8-0 No. 3278 *Franklin D. Roosevelt*, then based on the Mid Hants Railway, stands in the Up platform at Toddington during an evening photo shoot on the Gloucestershire Warwickshire Railway on July 20, 1996. ANTHONY BOWLES

LEFT: USATC No. 6046 poses in Froghall during a night photography session. FRED KERR

The Churnet Valley Railway, home to a pair of USATC S160 2-8-0s, echoed to the transatlantic sounds of the Second World War on March 12, 2016 when No. 6046 was hired by Lure of Steam charter organiser, Andrew Fowler, for a day of photography. No. 6046 (Baldwin 72080) hauled a goods consist that included military vehicles and support from enactors who brought a range of military vehicles. The day began at Kingsley & Froghall station where the enactors were introduced to the charter and began to familiarise themselves with the train and arrangements through the day. Some group members elected to follow the train by road using one of the group's Jeeps guided by a CVR member who appeared in period RAF costume. Oakamoor became the unloading point for training equipment. FRED KERR

first batch of 400, the GWR took 174, the LNER 168, the LMS 50 and the Southern six.

In Britain, the S160s had their own livery of matte light grey with silver letters and numbers. At first the locomotives said just 'USA' on their tenders, but later 'TRANSPORTATION CORPS' was added. Before handing back to the US Army, many of the S160s were repainted in gloss light grey. Effectively designed to be mass-produced 'on the cheap', the cutting of corners led to some problems in operating S160s. The axlebox grease lubricators were not very efficient, particularly when maintenance procedures lapsed or were delayed for operational war reasons, and so axleboxes often ran hot.

Furthermore, raking was poor for European standards, with the Westinghouse steam brake markedly insufficient owing to the long distance from the driver's valve and the brake cylinder.

TRAGEDY AT HONEYBOURNE

However, the biggest fault of the S160 was the crown stays in the firebox, coupled with only a single water gauge of an unreliable design, which was prone to blockage, misleading the crew into thinking that the water level was adequate, even though it was becoming dangerously low.

The bolts holding the crown stays were found to collapse under heat tension with low water levels and little warning, resulting in a boiler explosion. In a space of 10 months, three UK S160s suffered a collapse of the firebox crown, with the first leading to the death of a GWR fireman on No. 2403 on the Stratford-upon-Avon to Broadway and Cheltenham line, part of which is now the Gloucestershire Warwickshire Railway, in November 1943.

The 2.35pm Down goods train from Banbury to Margam, hauling No. 2403, was approaching the Honeybourne East Loop distant signal at about 11.55 pm when the crown of the steel firebox collapsed after shortage of water, and the train, which was travelling at about 25mph came to a stand 200yds before reaching the signal.

The guard, after ascertaining the cause of the stop, went back to protect his train, while the fireman, John William Sirrell, despite having been badly scalded, walked ahead nearly a mile to the Honeybourne East Loop signalbox to obtain assistance.

USATC 2-8-0 No. 6046 with a freight train carrying military vehicles and supplies passes Consall signalbox. FRED KERR

US Army personnel park their vehicles at Cheddleton station as No. 6046 sits in the platform.
FRED KERR

S160 No. 6046 heads a train loaded with military equipment on the Churnet Valley Railway.
FRED KERR

The signalman on duty, C Taylor, an ambulanceman of eight years standing, saw at once that the fireman was in a serious condition and made arrangements for him to be taken to Evesham Hospital after doing his best to apply first aid.

However, in the darkness and confusion on the footplate, the extent of his injuries had not been realised before he left the engine, and despite the signalman's effort, the fireman died later that day. Driver, Arthur Hill, luckily escaping with slight scalds on both wrists, did not have to go off duty. The disabled S160 was taken forward to Honeybourne, and the train proceeded on its journey at 4.36am.

The inspector who carried out the enquiry into this tragedy said that the footplate crew should not be blamed for the shortage of water, which led to the collapse of the firebox. "I am of opinion both Evans and Hill were, in fact, misled into thinking that the screw steam value was fully open, as the water gauge glass had given a false reading – a design anomaly."

Adding: "It must be attributed to the fact that the possibility of the screw steam valve being only partially open, and the serious effect thereof, had not hitherto been generally appreciated, as in the British practice a plug cock is used for this fitting.

"It will be seen, therefore, that plug cocks on water gauges have an advantage over screw valves, especially when the latter are in the hands of those who are not accustomed to them. This advantage is not sufficient, however, to justify drastic

alteration in that direction on the American engines, which are only temporarily in service in this country. As the men are becoming daily more accustomed to this type of engine, the risk of their being deceived by the water gauges should become remote."

Incidentally, the same signalbox was again the scene of a fatal accident when a Wellington bomber crashed near it on October 1944.

There were two further boiler explosions involving S160s in UK service.

The second explosion on January 12, 1944, occurred when No. 2352 was hauling an Ipswich to Whitemoor freight past Thurston.

The driver was injured, and the fireman was forced off the footplate by the explosion. The third explosion occurred in South Harrow tunnel on August 30, 1944 when No. 1707 was working a goods train from Neasden to Woodford.

The S160s worked much heavy goods traffic, but they had a high failure rate owing to hot axleboxes, tubeplate fractures, and leaking firebox arch tubes. The hot axleboxes were directly caused by the austerity measure of having grease lubricators on the axleboxes.

They were powerful and free-steaming locomotives, but their braking was poor when compared with British standards. A steam brake was used for the locomotive, but was woefully insufficient owing to the long distance from the driver's valve and the brake cylinder.

GATHERED FOR D-DAY

A second batch of 400 S160s were prepared for storage by USATC personnel at Ebbw Junction shed in the immediate build-up to D-Day.

After the Allied invasion of Normandy, the locomotives that had been deployed across Britain again began to be collected and refurbished at Ebbw Junction in preparation for shipment to Europe.

The explosion involving No. 1701 was not investigated fully because the S160s were being handed back to the US Army at the time. No. 1707 was eventually rebuilt, but did not arrive in Europe until after May 1945 and Hitler had been defeated.

Once on the continent, the primary purpose of S160s, was to act as part of the invasion force, but once territories had been liberated from Axis control, they were used on railways throughout Europe as replacements for war-damaged or destroyed locomotives.

Thirty went to Austria, the last of 80 in Czechoslovakia was withdrawn in 1972. France had 121 S160s, which were passed on to other countries, all 40 used in American and British zones in occupied German were sold to Hungary in 1947, the latter country acquiring 510, which became its Class 44, 244 going to Italy and some lasting in traffic until the early Sixties, Poland taking 575, the USSR ordering 200 examples, Turkey taking 50, Yugoslavia having 80 and northern Spain's Ferrocarril de Langreo buying six from the Alaska Railroad in 1958.

USATC S160 2-8-0s stored at Penrhos Junction in South Wales pending shipment to the continent following D-Day. Of strategic importance, they were kept under armed guard.

Somewhere under the rainbow... S160 No. 5197 on the turntable at Minehead during a visit to the West Somerset Railway on October 4, 2008. BEN SALTER*

The Keighley & Worth Valley Railway's 'Big Jim' S160 No. 5820 in action on October 23, 2015. BRIAN SHARPE

A total of 243 ended up in on the other side of the Mediterranean, being shipped there to aid General Patton's Operation Torch (the British-American invasion of French North Africa during the North African Campaign, which started on November 8, 1942.

After the Second World War, S160s were shipped to China, India and South Korea Asia under the United Nations Relief and Rehabilitation Administration. Many were later transferred to industrial operations including coal mines. China's last working example was taken out of service around 1997.

Bizarrely, S160s ended up being used by both sides during the Korean War.

No S160 was used on the UK network after the Second World War, but the Army retained Alco-built No. 71512 for use on the Longmoor Military Railway as WD 93257 *Carl R Gray Jr.*

S160s IN BRITAIN TODAY

At least 25 S160s have survived into preservation across the world, including six complete ones in the UK.

On the Churnet Valley Railway can be found USATC No. 5197 (Lima works number 8856) and No. 6046 (Baldwin No. 72080), which ran in Hungary for

Magyar Államvasutak or MÁV (Hungarian State Railways) as Class 411.

No. 5197 was exported to China in January, 1946. The S160s were classified as KD6 by the Chinese State Railways, and No. 5197 became KD6.463. It spent most of its working life in the Chinese coal industry around Fushun, before being withdrawn in the 1990s.

It was saved from scrap by UK preservationist, Derek Foster, in November 1995, who took it to the Llangollen Railway in North Wales where it was overhauled and returned to traffic in 1998 in USATC grey livery.

Offered for sale in 2001, Greg Wilson bought it and moved it to the Churnet Valley Railway, where it successfully operated for three years with guest visits to other heritage lines.

During the winter of 2004-05, at Ian Riley's Bury works, it underwent an intermediate mechanical overhaul, and a standard British air brake system was fitted. It re-entered service in June 2005, was repainted into USATC black, and operated both on its home line and other preserved railways until withdrawal for a full overhaul in December 2009.

No. 6046 (Baldwin No. 70280) was exported straight to France in 1945 to help with the war effort. Once its use with SNCF ended, it ended up in Hungary.

The S160s were classified as the MAV 411 class by the Hungarian State Railways, and 6046 became 411.144. Most of its working life was spent on industrial lines before

S160 2-8-0 No. 3278 *Franklin D. Roosevelt* heads a charter freight bound for Toddington between the two Didbrook bridges on the Gloucestershire Warwickshire Railway on July 20, 1996. ANTHONY BOWLES

withdrawal. It was formally preserved in the Hungarian National Collection, but after an administrative error, it was sent for scrap.

UK pilot, Martin Haines, stepped in to save it from being cut up, and imported it with the intention of restoring it to working order. Restoration began at Tyseley Locomotive Works, but it was sold as a kit of parts to Greg Wilson, owner of No. 5197, who took it to the CVR. He restarted its restoration in 2006, and on June 29, 2012, it moved under its own power for the first time in Britain.

On the Keighley & Worth Valley Railway can be seen 'Big Jim' No. 5820 (Lima No. 8758).

Built in 1945, it was shipped directly to Poland. After the war the locomotive was taken into stock by Poland State Railways and renumbered TR203-474.

It remained in Poland until withdrawal for preservation by the Polish Railway Museum in Warsaw.

Purchased by the KWVR, No. 5820 arrived at Haworth in November 1977 and entered service the following year still carrying the Polish livery. During this time the engine was re-liveried to USATC grey and chosen to appear in the feature film Yanks, filmed on location in Keighley.

Following withdrawal at the expiration of its boiler certificate, the engine underwent a thorough overall returning to service in February 2014, temporarily painted in BR unlined black, and fictitiously numbered 95820.

For the Easter holiday that year, No. 5820 regained its correct number and authentic USATC grey livery and is now regularly seen working trains along the branch.

No. 2253 (Baldwin No. 69496), which had worked for the LNER during the war, and was imported from Poland by locomotive owner Pete Best's Steam Powered Services Limited in 1992, ran on the North Yorkshire Moors Railway for seven years, covering 41,000 miles before boiler issues stopped the engine It has been repurchased by SPS.

After cosmetic restoration, it went on display at the Locomotion museum in Shildon, and is now being restored to working condition at AD Engineering in Stockton-on-Tees. Once running again, it will go on loan to Devon's Dartmouth Steam Railway for 10 years.

S160s are wholly appropriate to that line. Several were based at Newton Abbot and the type ran through to Kingswear.

At Tyseley Locomotive Works can be found No. 3278 *Franklin D. Roosevelt* (Baldwin No. 70430), which ran on the Mid Hants Railway in the 1990s.

At the Great Central Railway (Nottingham)'s Ruddington base, USATC No. 1631 (Alco No. 70284) is under restoration, with No. 2138 (Alco No. 70620) and the chassis of No. 2364 (Baldwin No. 69621) as a source of spares. All three were acquired from Hungary where they ran in service for MAV.

USATC S160 2-8-0 No. 3278, built in 1944 by Alco as works number 71533, approaches Toddington Yard with a train from Far Stanley on May 27, 1996. ANTHONY BOWLES

An S160 being unloaded in Normandy.

USATC No. 2253 out of traffic and parked in a siding on the North Yorkshire Moors Railway on January 30, 2008. JAMES RUSSELL

Yankees and pirates at the docks

Unlike the bigger S160 class, a series of US-built 0-6-0T shunting locomotives stayed on after the Second World War to operate on the UK national network, in some cases until the end of steam. Not only that, but the USATC S100s proved so popular that a new class of Western Region locomotives was based on them, and pirate copies began to be built in Eastern Europe!

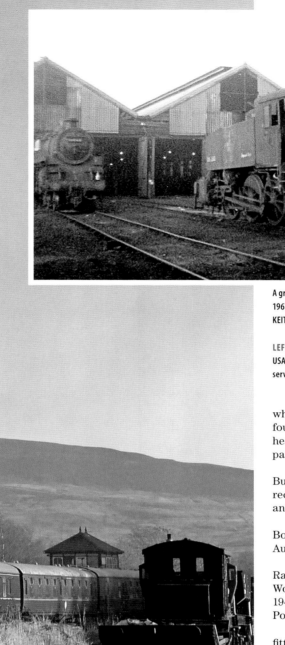

A grubby class member at Eastleigh locomotive depot in February 1967 during the last year of Southern Region steam. KEITH CHAMBERS*

LEFT: On loan to the Embsay & Bolton Abbey Steam Railway, USA dock tank No. 65/30065 raised a head of steam in passenger service on April 1, 2011. BRIAN SHARPE

A smaller class of locomotive built for the United States Army Transportation for use in the Second World War was the S100, designed by Col Howard G Hill in 1942.

A total of 382 were turned out by a series of manufacturers in the USA.

They arrived in the UK in 1943 in anticipation of D-Day, after which most were shipped to the continent.

They were painted USATC black with white numbering and 'Transportation Dept' lettering on the tank sides.

A few remained in store at Newbury racecourse having seen little use. Like other Big Four companies, the Southern Railway found itself short of locomotives after years of wartime austerity and sought to replace the E1, B4 and D1 tanks used in Southampton Docks.

The locomotives needed to have a short wheelbase to negotiate the tight curves found in the dockyard, but be able to haul heavy freight trains as well as full-length passenger trains in the harbour area.

SR Chief Mechanical Engineer Oliver Bulleid ran the rule over the S100s, and recommended that 14 were bought, plus another one for spares.

Other S100s went to the National Coal Board, the Longmoor Military Railway and Austin Motors.

Of the 15 acquired by the Southern Railway, 13 were built at the Vulcan Iron Works in Wilkes-Barre, Pennsylvania in 1942, with the other two coming from HK Porter of Pittsburgh.

Once in Southern hands, they were fitted with steam heating, vacuum ejectors, sliding cab windows, additional lamp irons and new cylinder drain cocks.

Further modifications became necessary once the locomotives started to enter traffic, including large roof-top ventilators, British-style regulators (as built they had US-style pull-out ones), three rectangular cab-front lookout windows, extended coal bunkers, separate steam and vacuum brake controls as well as wooden tip-up seats.

Telephones were later installed on the footplate to improve communication on the vast network of sidings at Southampton.

It took until November 1947 for the entire new class – which became known as 'Yankee tanks' – to be ready for work.

Before Nationalisation, the locomotives were painted in Southern black livery with Southern in Sunshine Yellow lettering. The lettering on the tank sides was changed to British Railways' during 1948 as a transitional measure. Finally, class members were painted in BR Departmental Malachite livery, with BR crests on the tank sides and numbers on the cabsides.

USA dock tank No. 30069 working at Southampton Docks on April 26, 1962. C HOGG/COLOUR-RAIL

Thirteen of the locomotives were renumbered in a single sequence from 61-73 by the Southern Railway but No. 4326 retained its earlier War Department number instead of being renumbered 74. The locomotive used for spares was not numbered.

After 1948 they were renumbered 30061-30074 by BR. Six examples were transferred to departmental use in 1962-63 and renumbered DS233-DS238.

They were used for shunting in Southampton Docks for 15 years and performed well. They were powerful, economical to operate and at first relatively easy to maintain. However, because they were basic machines turned out as cheaply as possible during the years of wartime austerity, age took its toll more quickly than might be expected.

Their steel fireboxes rusted and fatigued quickly, and in 1951 several

needed new ones. At the docks, they were replaced by British Rail Class 07 diesel-electric shunters, in 1962, when the first member of the class was withdrawn. The six departmental locomotives went to Redbridge Sleeper Depot, Meldon Quarry, Ashford wagon works (two locomotives) and Lancing Carriage Works (two locomotives).

Other survivors were used for informal departmental purposes such as steam heating at Southampton or shunting at

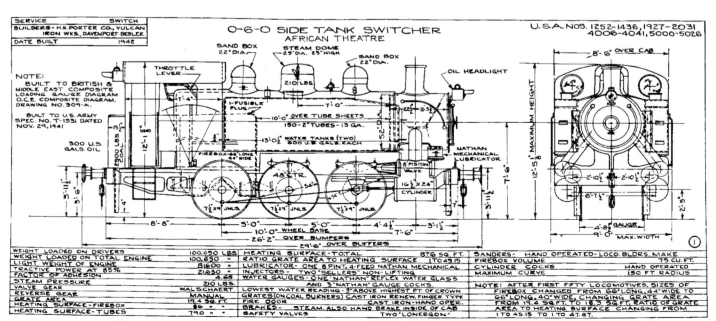

The original drawings for the USA S100 0-6-0T – a design that was copied in Eastern Europe.

No. 30073 at Eastleigh shed in August 1966. STEPHEN GILLETT*

Eastleigh Motive Power Depot before withdrawal. Nine examples remained in March 1967 and five of these survived until the end of steam on the Southern Region that year.

Examples of the class hold the distinction of being the last locomotives in steam on the Southern Region. Although the official date for the end of Southern steam is given as July 9, 1967, two S100 soldiered on until September that year in use as Ashford shed pilots.

Thankfully, the pair, Nos. 30065/DS237 and 30070/DS23830075, developed hot boxes while being towed to Cashmore's scrapyard in South Wales, and were dumped at Tonbridge. Too expensive to move by road for scrapping, the nascent Kent & East Sussex Railway intervened to buy them.

Two others survived: No. 30064, which ended up on the Bluebell Railway, and No. 30072, which was for a long time part of the Keighley & Worth Valley Railway fleet and is now undergoing an overhaul at the Ribble Steam Railway.

Many were bought by the railways of countries in which they served following D-Day, joining locomotive fleets of railways in France, Greece, Hungary, Turkey, Czechoslovakia, Yugoslavia and Iraq. Around 100 were bought by China and two ended up in the newly founded state of Israel.

Yugoslav State Railways Jugoslovenske Železnice acquired many examples and designated them Class 62. Typical of communist states, which paid little heed to Western design copyright, JŽ ordered several 'bootleg' copies from Duro Dakovi

of Slavonski Brod, Croatia. They differed from the USA originals in minor details, mainly in the use of plate frames instead of bar frames, resulting in a higher boiler pitch. That gave the steam pipes a shoulder instead of being straight, and requires smaller domes with a flatter top to fit JŽ's loading gauge. Both the old and new versions were known in Yugoslavia as the Class 62s.

The Polish TKh Ferrum 0-6-0Ts, which were built from 1947 onwards, were very much like the S100s. They have a similar outline but include various differences such as the use of two domes instead of three, driving on to the second axle instead of the third and a different cab.

Closer to home, Col Hill's design also impressed the last GWR Chief Mechanical Engineer, Frederick Hawksworth.

Having a large boiler but a short wheelbase, his 1500 class comprised the final Swindon-designed pannier tanks of all, and the entire class of 10 appeared after Nationalisation.

They were Hawksworth's most radical design; the very small footplate resembling the S100, several of which had been used by

USA 0-6-0T No. 72/30072, long owned by Richard Greenwood and an icon of the Keighley & Worth Valley Railway, was transferred to the Ribble Steam Railway for restoration after being sold to Andy Booth who has a fleet of hire locomotives. It is hoped that it will return to the KWVR to doublehead the heritage line's 50th anniversary train with Ivatt 2MT 2-6-2T No. 41241 in 2018. A new firebox is required. It is pictured inside the KWR's Oxenhope museum before its move to Lancashire. ROBIN JONES

S100 No. 30071 in service at Southampton Docks on August 25, 1957 K FAIREY/COLOUR-RAIL

USA dock tank No. 30072 shunting at Guildford yard in May 1963. HUGH LLEWELLYN*

USA dock tank No. 30074 shunting at the Bluebell Railway in the early 1980s. HEC TATE*

the GWR in South Wales during the Second World War.

The all-new 12ft 10in wheelbase chassis with outside cylinders and Walschaerts valve gear allowed the type to negotiate curves of 230ft radius. Designed for easy maintenance by the trackside, the outside valve gear and cylinders allowed easy access to working parts.

The lack of a running plate reflected the years of austerity in which they were built. There was extensive use of welded fabrication, also one of Hawksworth's developments to combat postwar shortages.

They had the same No. 10 boiler as the 94XX panniers tanks, and their weight – they were heavier than any other 0-6-0 built by the GWR – also limited their use to red routes.

However, the short wheelbase made them unsteady and unsuitable for fast running, one of the reasons why no more were built.

The first, No. 1500, appeared in June 1959, and the last Nos. 1506-9, in September that year. The first six in the series were allocated to Old Oak Common for shunting carriages to Paddington, while others served at sheds including Severn Tunnel Junction, Newport, Didcot, Cardiff Canton and Southall.

Historians continue to question the wisdom of building the class when some of them lasted little more than a decade in British Railways service. They were withdrawn between 1959-63, with three

of them, Nos. 1501, 1502 and 1509 being bought by the National Coal Board for use at Coventry Colliery.

The three were eventually bought as a job lot for preservation on the Severn Valley Railway in 1970, but because funds were tight, the purchase had to be funded by the reselling of two of them for scrap once they had been stripped of spare parts. That left just No. 1501, the sole-surviving example of the class, and a popular and reliable performer on the SVR today.

As the UK heritage railway movement mushroomed in the decades following the end of British Rail steam on the main line, and sources of locomotives such as Barry scrapyard dried up, enthusiast groups began to look overseas.

What if an imported Yugoslavian Class 62 could be slightly cosmetically modified to resemble one of the Southern Region examples?

In 1990, class members were still active throughout Yugoslavia and so a decision was made by a group of British enthusiasts to purchase one.

A suitable locomotive was located at the Store Steelworks near Ljubljana, in what is now Slovenia.

No. 62-669 was built by Djuro Djakovic as recently as 1960 and had been made redundant after only 25,000 miles in service.

Following a thorough examination, finance was raised on behalf of what was to become Project 62, named after the class, and No. 62-669 was purchased.

It was dismantled on site in order to ensure clearance through the alpine road tunnels and was transported overland from Slovenia to the Swanage Railway, where it was re-assembled and prepared for service.

After running for two years, more improvements were carried out in 1994, during a major overhaul. To enhance the link with the old Southern Railway, the owners decided that 62-669 would adopt malachite green livery and take on the next vacant number in the class sequence 30075.

Sadly, the locomotive suffered a major steam pipe failure in 1998 and was withdrawn from traffic. Dismantled at Swanage, it was moved by road to the East Somerset Railway in July 2002 and returned to traffic on July 7, 2004.

No. 30075 was relocated to the Mid Hants Railway in August 2009 and, following withdrawal after leaks in the inner firebox, was moved to Barrow Hill Roundhouse for repairs in February 2012.

In 2006, the opportunity arose to acquire a second Class 62, this time from Mittal Steel Zenica in Bosnia Herzegovina. No. 62-521 will be rebuilt to form the 16th Southern/BR USA Tank and has been numbered 30076.

On January 20, 2016, the Project 62 pair arrived at the new restoration base, Shillingstone station on the former Somerset & Dorset Joint Railway, and now the home of the North Dorset Railway Trust.

Even though No. 30075 is out of its

USA class No. 30065, a Kent & East Sussex Railway resident for nearly half a century, climbs the railway's 1-in-50 Tenterden bank with a Santa special on December 12, 2015. GEOFF COURTNEY

No. 30075 in steam at Ropley sidings on the Mid Hants Railway in 2010. TRAIN PHOTOS*

Frederick Hawksworth's class of 15XX pannier tanks was largely influenced by the design of the USA dock tanks. The sole survivor, No. 1501, is seen in full flight on its Severn Valley Railway home on September 22, 2012. LEWIS MADDOX

boiler ticket, smoke rose from its chimney on February 11 when a film crew from Brighton-based Pier Productions filmed sequences for a programme for BBC South about 1966, when services on the Somerset & Dorset system were withdrawn.

Project 62's locomotive liaison officer Dave Eburne-Brown produced smoke for the occasion by lighting a small quantity of coal within the smokebox and this was supplemented with oily rags just before he was filmed 'oiling up' the motion. General shots of No. 30075 were also taken and lamps bearing an S&D headcode were displayed along with a company crest.

Chrzanow built in 1954 and similar in many ways to the USA S100s TKh 0-6-0T No. 4015 worked at a steelworks at Ostrowiec in the south-east of Poland until withdrawal in 1991, when it was bought by enthusiasts and imported to Britain. It steamed again in 1998 after a £60,000 overhaul. Now named Karel after the Polish Pope John Paul II, it is seen arriving at Oldland Common with a service from Bitton on the Avon Valley Railway on December 27, 2012. Several TKhs have been imported to Britain by enthusiasts for use on heritage lines, because unlike virtually all other Polish standard gauge steam locomotives, they conform to the British loading gauge. HUGH LLEWELLYN

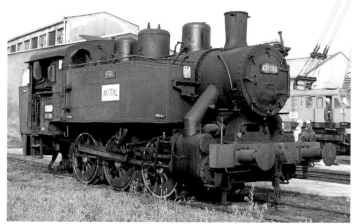

Class 62 No. 62-382 was still operational at Zenica in 2006. RICHARD WHITE/PROJECT 62

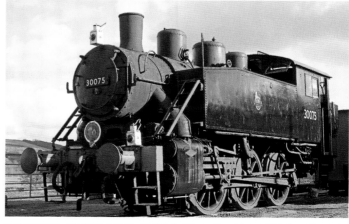

Steaming again – or maybe not, but No. 30075 looked the part for a February 11 filming assignment. PROJECT 62

The wartime railway they couldn't scrap

You won't find it in any directory of Britain's preserved railways, and it hasn't seen a train since the end of the Second World War. Yet an island in the Bristol Channel is home to a complete wartime railway network – one that may have fought on both sides.

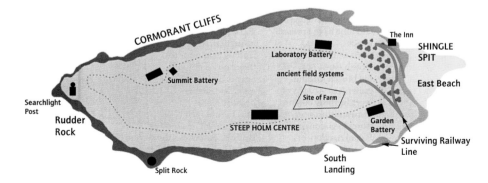

S teep and Flat Holm are two very unalike islands in the middle of the Bristol Channel. Outliers of Somerset's Mendip Hills, in character they are as their names indicate.

During the Second World War they each had their own railway networks.

Looking from a distance to be little more than lumps of grass-topped rock when viewed from either the English or Welsh shores, it seems barely conceivable that anyone would have ever wanted to visit either, let alone build railways there. Yet both have a history dating back thousands of years – indeed, it is believed that St Gildas wrote the first history of Britain while staying on Steep Holm in the sixth century.

Flat Holm, which has been part of Wales since the Norman Conquest, lost its line to the scrap men soon after it became

redundant. Yet Steep Holm proved too steep for the recovery men to tackle: quite simply, the time and expense that would be incurred in scaling its heights could never justify the reclamation of scrap rails and metal sleepers, never mind the safety aspects.

So, Steep Holm's railway is still there for

all to see – a perfect case of preservation, if only because nobody wants to lift its rusting tracks.

The Kenneth Allsop Memorial Trust, which has managed Steep Holm as a nature reserve in honour of the late broadcaster and naturalist since 1974, runs trips aboard the *Bristol Queen* from Knightstone

ABOVE: The Second World War railway track still in place on the zigzag incline path. The sleepers have been covered with soil to make it easier for the island's Honda Power Carrier to take supplies to the summit. ROBIN JONES

LEFT: Looking down the incline towards the South Landing. ROBIN JONES

INSET RIGHT: A memorial to the men who built the Second World War fortifications and the island railway. ROBIN JONES

THE ISLAND'S FOUR SECOND WORLD WAR SIX-INCH GUN BATTERIES WERE BUILT BY 930 PORT CONSTRUCTION AND REPAIR COMPANY OF THE ROYAL ENGINEERS AND THE PIONEER CORPS FOR THE ROYAL ARTILLERY IN THE DEFENCE OF FREEDOM, JULY TO OCTOBER 1941. THIS STONE IS A MEMORIAL TO ALL WHO SERVED ON STEEP HOLM AND IN THE FIXED DEFENCES (SEVERN). IT WAS UNVEILED ON THE OCCASION OF THE FIFTIETH ANNIVERSARY OF THE ISLAND'S FORTIFICATION

MAJOR DAVID BENGER
O/C 146 COAST BATTERY R.A.
RODNEY LEGG, WARDEN, STEEP HOLM ISLAND

Harbour at Weston-super-Mare on selected days.

The first question every visitor asks is how did this all-but-uninhabited lump of rock end up not only with its own railway – but two separate lines?

The answer lies in not one, but two, world wars.

Following the evacuation of the British Army from Dunkirk in 1940, Britain was placed on invasion alert. Fortifications were erected at every conceivable 'weak' point across the country, with special emphasis given to the southern coastline facing the English Channel. Other areas, however, were under potential threat, and the docks at Cardiff and Newport were particularly vulnerable to Luftwaffe raids.

The Holms were not only the guardians of the shipping lane leading up the estuary to the Port of Bristol, but also stood below the flight path of bombers. They also afforded protection to the Atlantic convoys, which would rendezvous in the Bristol Channel.

Somerset was also considered particularly vulnerable to a potential invasion because of the flat fens, over which an invading force might quickly make ground, and so it was turned into a

fortress, bristling with pillboxes and gun emplacements. Many of these can be seen around the coast today at places such as Berrow.

Both Steep and Flat Holm were taken over by the Army and again turned into fortresses. I say 'again' because both islands were already covered by an extensive series of fortifications dating from the 1860s.

It was then that unfounded fears of the intentions of the French Emperor Napoleon III, a nephew of Napoleon Bonaparte, prompted the British government under Lord Palmerston to commission a new chain of defensive forts to be built around the coast of southern England.

Thankfully no shot was fired in anger. In fact, Napoleon III was rather fond of England and spent his last years in exile here after his country's humiliating defeat in the Franco-Prussian War of 1870-71.

The island forts, including the barracks on Steep Holm, were eventually vacated in 1902.

Steep Holm's 10 massive 7in muzzle-loading cannons were left for the scrap merchants; however, because of the topography of the island, no one considered their salvage worthwhile, and nine have

survived intact.

As air raids began on British cities, Mk. VII 6in breech-loading guns up to 40 years old were hurriedly taken from ammunition stores in Cardiff for use on the islands by the Royal Artillery Regiment.

A contingent of Indian Army soldiers with mule teams arrived, the animals carrying much of the equipment up the incline path from East Beach to the island's summit.

Building supplies and equipment were brought in by tank-landing craft before the construction of a jetty at Last Beach, an essential facility.

The sheer extent of the planned island fortifications meant that the Indian Sappers' mule trains using the single narrow incline path up from the beach would prove inadequate if the gun emplacements were to be completed in time to be effective against the growing number of air raids.

As far as the military engineers were concerned, the only answer was to build a railway.

Track materials, which had been held in store at the Longmoor Military Railway since the First World War, were brought to the island.

Somerset's Steep Holm island, as viewed from the huge shingle spit, which appears off East Beach at low water. Believe it or not, it once had its own railway network. ROBIN JONES

The salty air of the Severn estuary is not good for metal sleepers. ROBIN JONES

The site of one of the winding houses that hauled the trains up the zigzag incline railway. Today it is the sole path to the island summit. ROBIN JONES

Landing on Steep Holm today can only be done at precise states of the tide. ROBIN JONES

A rockfall blocks the line on the zigzag path. KAMT

It is generally believed that the components had been previously used in trench lines on the Western Front. David Benger, battery commander on Flat Holm from 1941-44, said that he understood that the rail at least was of German origin and had been 'captured' from the Huns in 1918. So, here was an example of German military hardware from one war being used against its country of origin in the second!

Royal Engineers worked round the clock to build a 120ft-long girder landing jetty, standing waist deep in the freezing brown Severn sea to complete it, as a permanent harbour that was not reliant on the precarious state of tides was of utmost priority.

Then a formation had to be created to take the railway from the new military harbour up the zigzag incline path to the plateau at the island's summit. This path is a natural incline in the carboniferous limestone strata which, as a result of primeval earth movements, spectacularly tilts at 30° to the horizontal. It is also the only way up from East Beach to the 'habitable' summit of Steep Holm, which was once home to a small 12th-century

colony of monks and later a farmhouse.

A fisherman's cottage, and a pub dating from 1832 stood just above East Beach – drawing its trade from sailors on passing ships waiting in the lanes for the tide so they could enter the port of Bristol – were largely blasted away by explosives laid by 930 Port Construction and Repair Company to make way for the railway.

The pub's landlord in the mid-19th century, Fred Harris, who had skirmishes with Somerset magistrates over the opening hours, found himself at the centre of a claim for damages in 1858. Teacher Ann Besozzi took out a civil action against him for injuries suffered when she was felled by an almighty blow to the back.

She looked up to see a huge grizzly bear, chained to a kennel inside the premises, which Fred had obtained in exchange for his guard dog.

A fellow visitor succeeded in fighting off the bear with his umbrella, which was broken into pieces in the process. Miss Besozzi required extensive treatment for severe injuries. In his defence, Harris said that the bear regularly played with his children like an ordinary family dog and

was a docile creature.

The railway, comprising rails fixed to metal sleepers, was built in 1941 as a cable-operated incline line in separate sections laid on the zigzag path. It was constructed to 1ft 11½in gauge, the same as the Ffestiniog Railway and numerous other narrow gauge lines on the mainland.

At the top of each of the three sections, a set of points and a diesel-operated winch house were installed.

Trucks were loaded on to the jetty using a diesel crane. They were coupled together to the front truck. The train was then hauled up the inclines by each winch in turn, reversing at the end of each zigzag section.

The 1-in-2/3 gradient of the path caused problems for the trucks, never mind humans. Each truck had an 8cwt capacity. The profiles of the rails were accordingly bent in at least five places with oxy-acetylene torches to provide greater adhesion.

At the top of the incline, a long-forgotten diesel locomotive, possibly a Hunslet 0-4-0, hauled the wagons to the various construction sites and sidings around

A sketch of anti-aircraft guns in action on adjacent Flat Holm, which had its island military railway removed for scrap after the Second World War. ROBIN JONES

Hated with a vengeance by Second World War soldiers, the Victorian barracks now house a shop and dining facilities for visitors and double up as the island's post office. ROBIN JONES

The interior of the Victorian barracks today. ROBIN JONES

The Second World War Meccano-style pier at East Beach being demolished in 1946. This is the only known picture of the island railway in its operational days. Only the rusting pier stanchions survive today. Several of the trucks are seen on the railway line. KAMT

A set of wheels from an island railway truck are displayed inside the museum, which is next to the barracks. ROBIN JONES

the plateau, as was the case on the sister railway on Flat Holm, former sergeant Joe Walford later recounted. Other reports said that the wagons on the summit line were either pulled by mules or pushed by hand. The full extent of the track, believed to have been about two-thirds of a mile, remains unclear.

Once operational, the line carried vast quantities of sand and cement for the military building sites.

A new set of four-gun batteries superseded the Palmerston-era originals and searchlight positions, generator houses and a battery observation post were also constructed at different points around the summit of the 256-ft high island.

After the emplacements had been finished and the heavy guns delivered, much of the rail 'network' on the top of the island became redundant and was lifted, with Nissan huts being built on part of the formation. The incline section, however, remained in use for the delivery of ammunition and general supplies.

Fears that rough weather or storm surges would render the East Beach jetty unusable led to a second landing stage

being built below the cliffs to the south.

South Landing, as it was called, was also served by a separate winch-operated railway linking it to the path that circuits the summit of the island, although this line appears to have been seldom, if ever, used. With care, in dry weather, visitors can follow that path and the second railway today.

At one stage more than 200 soldiers were based on Steep Holm, preparing the guns for action at any time of the day.

Parachute mines dropped by Nazi planes in the Bristol Channel were often seen floating in the waters off the island, and several ships from Avonmouth were blown up by them.

Occasionally, German bombers flew low past Steep Holm on their way to Cardiff and, frustratingly, the island's anti-aircraft guns could not be lowered sufficiently to hit them.

Wartime conditions on the island were said to be very harsh, with an acute lack of water (a washing bowl had to he shared by 12 men) a typhoid outbreak, a ban on eating seagulls' eggs for risk of infection, and blackout conditions which led to several

men falling over the cliffs, not to mention the often-inhospitable channel climate.

Soldiers who were ferried over to the island for tours of duty cheered loudly when the sea became too choppy for them to land and they had to be taken back to Cardiff.

It was not always Cardiff that took a pounding from bombers. Weston-super-Mare emerged as a prime target on June 28, 1942, just days after the News Chronicle had run a front-page splash with the boastful headline 'Weston does not know there is a war on'.

Despite wartime austerity, holidaymakers continued to visit Weston and the hot summer that year brought the crowds back: unlike most other beaches, Weston's main sandy beach was not mined or protected by rows of barbed wire. A display of military hardware was staged on the sea front for munitions factory workers from all over Britain and the newspaper carried a photograph of the event.

That paper's front page turned out be a red rag to a bull.

While most air raids over the Holms had come from the Somerset direction, the one

The start of the incline path over which the military railway ran, with the ruined pub to the right. ROBIN JONES

This by-then derelict fisherman's cottage was partially blown up by Army engineers when laying the railway. The remains were used as a pigsty to supplement Army rations during the war. KAMT

A Victorian cannon lies on top of the island inside the battery built for it. As with the railway, scrap men did not consider reclamation economically justifiable. ROBIN JONES

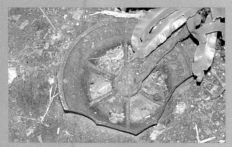

A pulley wheel from the zigzig incline railway. ROBIN JONES

A pile of rusting rails that were once part of Steep Holm's military railway. Were they of First World War German origin? ROBIN JONES

Too big to move, this Victorian cannon was simply buried beneath the concrete base of a Second World War battery. ROBIN JONES

Steep Holm's sister island Flat Holm also had a similar wartime railway, although it was removed after the end of the war because the scrap men had greater ease of access. FLAT HOLM PROJECT

that began that evening came unexpectedly from the sea. Air sirens were never sounded as the town was left totally unprepared, and the inhabitants did not even have time to scurry into their Anderson shelters.

Air raids from the West had not been anticipated: the distinctive white far end of Weston's Grand Pier was not camouflaged and it gave the Nazi pilot, duly aided by a glorious full moon, an added navigational bonus. Around 100 high-explosive bombs and 1000 incendiaries were dropped on the resort over two nights, several planes flying so low that they passed streets at the height of first-floor windows machine-gunning everything below.

While initially released figures put the death toll at 102 with 400 more injured, many locals believed the true numbers were much higher.

After the raids, Nazi sympathiser, William Joyce, nicknamed Lord Haw-Haw, who broadcast German propaganda nightly to Britain on Radio Hamburg, gloated: "I presume Weston knows there is a war on."

However, following D-Day in June 1944, the threat of Nazi invasion quickly diminished and all defence units were run down. Steep Holm was no exception and closed down late that year.

German prisoners of war were used to dismantle much of the fortifications including the East Beach jetty. Captured German NCO Max Hemming later remarked that the railway outlived the guns and searchlights, and his group not only used the line to carry supplies but passengers too!

The weight of the trucks was all that was needed to take them back down, with a brake on the winch acting as a safeguard, the PoWs found to their delight. Once, however, when nobody bothered to operate the brake, a truck ran down out of control, left the track and somersaulted on to the beach.

It seems that became the fate of other wagons, for while none today survive intact, a set of wheels was found off South Landing in 1977, and three more sets were salvaged from the sea off the western end of the island during a very low tide seven years later.

After Germany's defeat, it was the turn of Lord Haw-Haw to get his comeuppance. Shot in the backside by British troops during his arrest, the bullet had to be removed by a Dr Corcos – a Weston general practitioner who was only too aware of the casualties inflicted on his hometown. Joyce was later hanged for treason.

Abandoned by the military after 1944, and unwanted by the scrap men, the little railway was left to rust.

When the Kenneth Allsop Memorial Trust took over the island, one of the first tasks was to clear vegetation from the incline path. The Department of the Environment also advised that the railway track should stay intact because of its historic importance.

However, while the possibility was

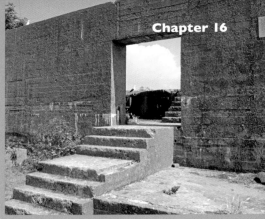

The huge concrete batteries at the eastern end of the island. ROBIN JONES

tempting for many reasons, it was realised any restoration of the line to working order would immediately place it in potential conflict with pedestrians. A runaway truck on a cable-hauled railway would take no prisoners on the narrow incline. As there is no realistic alternative path for visitors, the railway must therefore stay closed.

In recent times the railway track has been partially buried to allow the trust's Honda Power Carrier to use the incline without risk of its caterpillar tracks becoming damaged. Burial is also limiting the corrosive power of the salt air, which is already visibly taking its toll on many of the metal sleepers.

However, it would be brilliant if the trust was to restore a part of the line, maybe a winding house and a set of points at the end of a zigzag section, for static display, and perhaps this will happen when precious funds permit.

Yet it is all but certain that this forgotten but fascinating outpost of railway heritage will never see train movements again, and through necessity, is set to remain dormant until the effects of the elements taken their final toll.

With humans occupying it only during day trips, and there being no permanent residency, seagulls are the undisputed masters of the 63-acre island now – and they let visitors know it.

If you inadvertently approach their nests or chicks, which are to be found in the middle of the island summit's footpaths – there are no natural predators, and they breed anywhere without fear – you will be told in no uncertain terms you are not welcome. The standard practice is to dive at you directly from the front or rear, and then apply wing uplift seconds before contact, so you just feel the jet stream from the ferocious flapping passing fractionally over your head.

The deafening shrieks of tens of thousands of seagulls that make the island their sanctuary quickly invoke Alfred Hitchcock's The Birds at every step. Indeed, Steep Holm is a world apart from the mainland civilisation in so many respects, and as such is an experience to be prized.

Then there are the alexanders, a yellow-flowering herb popular as a celery substitute in medieval times. When you visit in early spring, it seems that the plant has taken over almost every square inch. To walk round the island you have to hack your way through alexanders several feet high. Their seeds get everywhere, inside your clothes, up your nose, in your mouth. You live, breathe and eat alexanders while you visit the island, and never want to see one or sense their unmistakeable aroma ever again!

* Anyone wishing to visit Steep Holm and see its unique railway relics is invited to contact the Kenneth Allsop Memorial Trust to make prior bookings, which are essential.
Telephone 01934 521725 or
visit www.steepholm.org.uk or
email steepholmbookings@fsmail.net

The island pub that was partially demolished to make way for the railway. A harbour built at the same time as the inn was washed away in 1860. ROBIN JONES

Much of the South Landing 'branch' is still intact, visible, and walkable with care. ROBIN JONES

The top of the South Landing incline, near where trucks would have been loaded, this is when the 'second' Steep Holm railway would have been brought into use. ROBIN JONES

The winch at the top of the South Incline. ROBIN JONES

A 40mm Bofors anti-aircraft gun. Six were positioned on Steep Holm during the Second World War. ROBIN JONES

The track on the second leg of the zigzag path with a set of original truck wheels. These had been rescued from the mud of the lower foreshore. KAMT

War on the STREETS

Heritage railways are a splendid stage for events such as wartime weekends. However, Crich Tramway Village can offer a different steel wheels perspective on the Forties – by re-creating life on the Home Front in typical city streets of the era.

A busy day ahead as the city prepares for a military parade, with Leeds Car 345 packed with spectators. MALCOLM WRIGHT

The village of Crich in Derbyshire has enjoyed a long love affair with steel wheels on rails.

It all began the George Stephenson, the 'Father of the Railways' who built the mineral railway to link the local limestone quarry to the new North Midland Railway at Ambergate.

His railways unusually were built to metre gauge – nobody knows exactly why he chose that size, but it has been speculated that it had something to do with the Dutch labourers hired in to do the job, who would have been familiar with metric measurements.

We all know about *Rocket* – hailed as the first 'modern' steam locomotive – and Stephenson's Liverpool & Manchester Railway – the world's first inter-city line –

TOP: A military parade passes 1912-built London Passenger Transport Board Car 1622, an example of the 'rehabilitated' E1 London trams of the Thirties. MALCOLM WRIGHT

Leeds Car 180 was built in 1931 by Brush Electrical Machines, and is sometimes referred to as a showboat tramcar because of the extraordinary amount of lighting. CTM

RIGHT: Top brass escorted by a police motorcyclist. MALCOLM WRIGHT

but at Crich, without exerting a tiny fraction of the mental energy involved in both of those globe-changing projects, he oversaw the construction of what is believed to be the world's first metre-gauge line. Although that gauge never took off in Britain, apart from a few industrial lines around the Northamptonshire ironstone quarries, it became huge on the continent and beyond.

Stephenson's mineral railway had passed into history long before the site became acquired for a very different kind of railway.

After the Second World War, many of the street tramways that had provided essential passenger services in Britain's cities began closing down, firstly in some cases giving way to the trolleybus, and then the infinitely more versatile motor bus.

The phasing out and replacement of trams by diesel buses or trolleybuses started in London around 1935, when many trams and sections of track and ancillary equipment were nearing the end of their useful life. Such replacements continued until hostilities stopped the conversion programme in June 1940, leaving only the South London trams and the routes that went through the Kingsway subway into North London.

After the Second World War, shortages of steel and electrical machinery were cited as reasons for not investing in maintenance, while services ran at a loss. The 1948 nationalisation of electricity suppliers removed access to cheap electricity for those tramways that owned their local power company.

ABB Valentine, one of the five full-time members of the London Transport Executive, viewed trams as a major cause of road congestion, which could be eradicated by the introduction of buses, with the added aesthetic benefit of doing away with overhead wires and their noisy operation. Also, the capital's housing developments were too far away from tram routes, with little prospect of those in existence being extended.

The first major British city to completely abandon its trams was Manchester, where all services had ended by January 1949. London's last trams ran in the early hours of July 6, 1952 with crowds gathering to see the last enter New Cross Depot. Following the closure of London's tram system, the Feltham trams were mostly sold to Leeds where they continued in service until the abandonment of that city's trams in 1959.

The last city system to close was Glasgow Corporation Tramways in

Glasgow Corporation Tramways Car 812 dates from 1900 when it was built as an open-top tram. It was given a top cover with open balconies a decade later and platform vestibules two years after that. ROBIN JONES

Local defence volunteers line up on the tram track for inspection. TIM STANGER

Stopping at one of the museum's tramstops is Leeds Car 399, which was built at the city's Kirkstall Works, and entered service in 1925. It was the second passenger tram to arrive at Crich but needed a lengthy restoration and did not return to service until 1991. CRT

Leeds enclosed double-decker No. 345 was built in 1921 but was taken out of service early because of poor bodywork and became a carpenters' tea shed at a Leeds depot. One of the first cars at Crich, its restoration to full working order was completed in 2006. CRT

Soldiers march to war. TIM STANGER

A Scout meets his officer heroes. TIM STANGER

1962. From the 'first generation of street tramways, only the Blackpool Tramway survive, maintaining an extensive and much-loved system, which includes some street running in Blackpool, and a long stretch of segregated track to nearby Fleetwood.

Postwar buses were cheaper to buy and maintain, and it was claimed that they gave a smoother ride and a faster journey than prewar trams.

Just as with the imminent demise of steam railways, visionary enthusiasts began to look at preserving items of rolling stock for posterity.

A group of enthusiasts on a farewell tour

of Southampton Tramways in August 1948 decided to purchase one of the open-top trams on which they had ridden. For the sum of £10 they got No. 45, and then came up with the idea of a working museum devoted to tramcars.

In 1955, the Tramway Museum Society was formed, and after scouring the country for a suitable site, four years later the derelict quarry at Crich was decided upon, where members of the Talyllyn Railway Preservation Society were recovering track from Stephenson's mineral railway.

The society leased and later purchased part of the site and buildings and slowly amassed a collection of tramcars on

Squaddies and their Jeep. TIM STANGER

Crich Tramway Museum has built up a superb collection of street furniture over the years. Nowadays best known by far as the Tardis in the science fiction series Dr Who, police boxes were introduced in Britain in the Twenties, for constables to keep in contact with a central police station. In 1929, a decision was made to introduce them to London, and by 1937, 700 were installed. Next to it stands a Bundy clock, which provided a reliable method of time recording for the tram routes. ROBIN JONES

Here comes the military police! MALCOLM WRIGHT

one site. Realising that tramcars did not run in quarry landscapes, in 1967 it was decided to create a series of street scenes. Members started collecting items of street furniture and complete buildings, not only as frontage for 'genuine' streets, but also as accommodation for the museum's rapidly expanding collections of books, photographs and archives.

And so what, for years, was dubbed the National Tramway Village was born.

As with restored railways, the street scenes are capable of providing backdrops for a wide variety of settings, not least of all the Forties, which for most British cities was the last great decade of the trams.

Hundreds of re-enactors performing roles from Winston Churchill to service personnel, US army and airforce staff, Home Guard volunteers and French Resistance fighters fill the streets, and some of the trams are fitted with black-out masks, anti-blast netting on the windows and blue-coloured lamps. Visitors who dress in Forties attire are offered discounted admission rates. Once inside the gates, you're given an old penny to ride on the trams all day.

Youngsters can take part in boot camps and there are also evacuee scenarios.

Rita's Tearoom offers wartime fayre

and the museum's Red Lion public house serves drinks while visitors can join in with traditional pub games of the period.

Historic wartime road and military vehicles are on show and at some events, a Second World War aircraft such as a Spitfire has been displayed outside the Assembly Rooms.

A Forties dance is held on Saturday evenings with entertainers, singers and musicians taking centre stage.

Not only is Crich Tramway Village a brilliant place to find out about a 'lost' slice of urban transport history but it's a valuable educational resource too.

Built in 1936, Liverpool Corporation Passenger Transport Car 869 was sold to Glasgow in 1954, from where it was withdrawn in 1960. Liveried green and white, it is referred to as the 'Green Goddess'.

The police escort exchanges words with a bystander during a lull in proceedings. MALCOLM WRIGHT

Fraternising with the local ladies. MALCOLM WRIGHT

First of the class: Q1 No. C1 as it appeared in a maker's photograph in 1942. THE RAILWAY MAGAZINE

The Q1 Bulleid's 'Ugly Duckling'

No Second World War locomotive design encapsulated wartime austerity to the extent of Oliver Bulleid's Q1 heavy freight 0-6-0.

Bulleid's streamlined Pacifics were marked for their flamboyance, whereas the Q1 were no-frills pared-to-the-bone out-and-out workhorses which, sometimes compared with a sequence of dustbins on wheels, would never win any beauty contests.

When Bulleid came up with the highly functional but nonetheless innovative design, he had in mind the intensive freight turns experienced during wartime on the Southern Railway.

In 1939, the company's Home Counties lines were largely electrified, and with the clouds of war looming, there were cries for a modern freight locomotive.

The most up-to-date class available to the SR was Richard Maunsell's Q 0-6-0s, which first appeared in 1938, but their design harked back to the late Victorian era.

The SR needed more, whether it liked it or not. It suddenly found itself in the front line, both defending the nation from invasion and supplying British troops on the battlefield on the continent. A locomotive with a high tractive effort capable of hauling the heaviest troop and military supply train was what was needed.

Hailed as the ultimate development of the British 0-6-0 freight engine, the 40 Q1s were capable of hauling trains that were normally allocated to much bigger types by other Big Four companies.

Popular nicknames for the class included Biscuit Tins, Biscuit Barrels, Charlies, Clockworks, Coffee Pots, Frankensteins and Ugly Duckings – probably more than other class of locomotive.

Bulleid, who replaced Maunsell in late 1937, took into account the impending wartime austerity regime and incorporated the minimum amount of raw materials, removing all unnecessary cosmetic features and any running plate and splasher, and came up with the most powerful 0-6-0 ever to run on the UK network. Weight-saving principles came to the forefront: because a Q1 weighed less than 90 tons, it could be used over more than 97% of the SR routes.

Exerting 30,000lb at 85% boiler pressure, the Q1s had at 27 sq ft, the largest fire grate area of any British 0-6-0, weighing 14 tons less than a comparable engine.

Also, their cylindrical shape allowed them to be driven through a coach-washer for cleaning at a time when manpower could not be spared.

Furthermore, they were lagged with a glass-fibre insulation material that was cheap and plentiful during the war years. However, it could not support any weight,

Q1 0-6-0 No.C1 at Sheffield Park on the Bluebell Railway in August 1999. HUGH LLEWELLYN*

The first and sole-surviving Bulleid Q1, No. 33001, painted in Southern Railway livery as C1 and now displayed in the Great Hall at the National Railway Museum at York. ROBIN JONES

and therefore a separate casing was required, and as with the Merchant Navy Pacifics, the boiler rings were adapted to lend the lagging the support needed.

The boiler design was based upon that of the Lord Nelson class, and the firebox used the same throatplate and backplate.

The first batch of 20 was built at Brighton Works, the first appeared in 1942, and the second 20 at Ashford.

Mainly freight engines, they were sometimes used on passenger trains on secondary routes.

British Rail gave the Q1s the power classification 5F.

Bulleid's 'Ugly Duckings' were a major Second World War success story for the Southern, and after the conflict ended, they provided many more years of service.

The first withdrawals began in 1963, as a result of modernisation, with Nos. 33006, 33020 and 33027 the last in service in 1966.

The important role the class played in the war, meant that No. 33001, the first

Q1, was saved for the National Collection following its withdrawal in 1964.

After working on the Bluebell Railway for 27 years (during which time it was overhauled twice), in 2004, with its boiler ticket expired, and no prospect of a fast-

track overhaul in the workshops, it was taken to the National Railway Museum at York where it remains on display in the Great Hall. The museum has indicated that the Q1 could return to the line in the future for display or another term of running.

Q1 No. 33016 at Feltham shed on May 11, 1959. BEN BROOKSBANK*

War in the COTSWOLDS

There can be few settings as idyllic as the Cotswolds with its rolling hills and yellowstone villages. Yet for one weekend each year the black clouds loom overhead as the Gloucestershire Warwickshire Railway holds its acclaimed Wartime in the Cotswolds event.

Auxilliary Fire Service officers John Print (left) and Phil Harbron ensure that Toddington station's telephone box is well protected. IAN CROWDER

One of the biggest events in the calendar of the revivalists who re-opened the section of the GWR Stratford-upon-Avon to Cheltenham main line via Laverton and Cheltenham Raceourse, and now mounting a final push to reach the tourist honeypot of Broadway, is the annual Forties event.

It attracts thousands of visitors; uniforms and Forties clothing are very much in evidence as volunteers, re-enactors and members of the public enter into the spirit of the occasion.

The 2016 event held on April 23-24, was marked by fine weather and, of course, a visit by King George VI who, as befits royalty, attracted large crowds, never mind the steam trains and glorious scenery.

He visited the Northamptonshire Home Guard and Tail End Charlie's RAF & FAA re-enactment group, as well as making a speech, complete with stuttering delivery, at Toddington.

Escorted by Field Marshall Montgomery he roused the good people of Winchcombe to do their bit for the war effort.

A vintage bus service was laid on to ferry passengers from Winchcombe station to the town centre, which lies the best part of half a mile away.

Other attractions included the acclaimed RAF Plotting Room demonstration, a Forties beauty salon, military and period vehicles, an air raid shelter experience, local people knitting for the war effort and 'digging for victory', with the Home Guard out in force. Shops had themed displays with staff wearing period clothing, many with their windows taped and sandbagged in case of an air raid.

There were solemn moments, for example, when Rev Eric Umpleby conducted a short but moving service in the presence of the King reminding us all why heritage railways run events of this sort; not just for nostalgia but to remember those who gave their all for our freedom.

Gloucestershire Warwickshire Railway spokesman, Ian Crowder, said: "Britain was at war, but it was also a time when the country was buoyed up with camaraderie, music and everyone looking out for each other."

TOP: GWR heavy freight 2-8-0 No. 2807 – dating from 1905 the oldest Great Western locomotive in steam – has seen service in two world wars, and now sees service at events such as War in the Cotswolds. This peaceful 2015 scene witnesses the locomotive drifting into Gotherington station under the watchful eye of the Worcestershire Home Guard. G/WR

Ray the Spiv is apprehended for attempting to flog his ill-gotten gains including hard-to-get silk underwear and stockings on the train. Yet judging by the lipstick on his cheek, someone appreciated his efforts, even if the police didn't. This is just one of a number of scenarios played out on the trains for the entertainment of visitors. G/WR

At delightful rural Gotherington the privately owned station grounds are opened up for occasions such as War in the Cotswolds, where encampments are set up, including the Northamptonshire Home Guard. G/WR

Left to right are King George VI (played superbly by Paul Eastwood – even down to the well-managed stutter); Viscount Montgomery, and Mark Evans of the railway's event-organising team. King George and 'Monty' had just delivered speeches to a packed and very respectful audience. IAN CROWDER

Colin Bourdie as George Formby gives a superb performance to a packed and appreciative audience of civvies and military personnel. IAN CROWDER

Join in on the train with the Memory Lane singers from Devon. G/WR

This Forties boutique is run by Lady She of Sheunique Vintage who exhibited a range of Forties fashions and accessories as well as doing make-up and hair makeovers. IAN CROWDER

The Channel Islands apart, no German locomotive ever ran on British soil during the Second World War, or in the earlier conflict for that matter. However, a handful of steam engines built for the German war effort have appeared on our heritage lines.

The enemy WITHIN

It was not just the British and the French who had extensive trench railway systems on the Western Front. The Germans developed their own system of narrow gauge field railways, Feldbahnen, to rapidly transport large quantities of supplies, heavy equipment and troops.

The Germans too saw that narrow gauge vehicles and track could be easily portable and could be quickly moved as the location of the front line changed.

Henschel 0-8-0T No. 15968 of 1918 (Heeresfeldbahn No. 1091) steams into Toddington on the North Gloucestershire Railway on April 24, 2016, during the Gloucestershire Warwickshire Railway's Wartime in the Cotswolds event. IAN CROWDER

TOP: Old First World War enemies now firm friends – Baldwin No. 778 doubleheads with Henschel 0-8-0T No. 1091 at the Leighton Buzzard Railway's 90th anniversary gala on May 31, 2009. CLIFF THOMAS

A type of locomotive referred to as a 'Feldbahn design' is normally the standard German Army Field Railway (Deutscher Feldbahn, DFB) locomotive originally introduced in 1907.

A total of 2473 Feldbahn locomotives or 'Brigadeloks' were built by 14 different manufacturers up to the end of the First World War. The most well-known manufacturers are Henschel & Sohn of Cassel, and Orenstein & Koppel.

The remarkable aspect of these tank engines is their flexible 0-8-0 wheelbase, whereby the leading and trailing axles are arranged with exaggerated sideplay and an ability to "steer" round sharp curves.

After the war many almost-new locomotives were sold to industrial users in a variety of countries. Fifteen were shipped out to the Sena Sugar Estates at Luabo on the banks of the Zambezi in Mozambique. The Sena Sugar Estates extended over a vast area and employed tens of thousands of workers.

In late 1998, traction engine enthusiast and Warwickshire quarry owner, Peter Court, imported a job lot of 19 steam locomotives from Sena, and the following year went back for three more. The shipment included no fewer than 14 Feldbahn 0-8-0Ts.

His was the biggest importation of steam locomotives to Britain since the consignments of engines shipped over from the USA during the Second World War.

At first stored in a Warwickshire farmyard, the Feldbahns were offered for sale to enthusiast groups, and there were willing takers. Some have been returned to steam, while others are still being restored.

One First World War Henschel 0-8-0T now in regular heritage railway service is No. 15968 of 1918 (Heeresfeldbahn No. 1091).

It is fitted with front and rear axles of the Klien-Lindner type that allows the wheels to move laterally and radially with respect to the axle itself. This allows the locomotive to traverse curves of tighter radius than would be possible with rigid axles – excellent for Front Line duties.

It is now running on the 2ft gauge North Gloucestershire Railway, which runs for a mile from the Gloucestershire Warwickshire Railway's Toddington station.

Not one of the Mozambique imports, No. 1091 was obtained from Naklo Sugar Factory in Poland by a group of members and arrived at Toddington in October 1985. It has now been restored to the original condition as supplied to the German army and has run on the Leighton Buzzard Railway on one occasion double heading with Baldwin 4-6-0T No. 778, built in the USA for use on the Allied side. It was arranged by the Greensand Railway Museum Trust as a 'hand of friendship' gesture.

German-built Feldbahn 0-8-0T No. 2023 awaits restoration at Stonehenge Works on the Leighton Buzzard Railway, which acquired it in 2014. Built by Lokomotivfabrik Krauss as No. 7455, after the First World War, it was used on the sugar beet railway at Maizy in northern France. It moved to a sand quarry in Variscourt in 1964 before being preserved in 1970. MERVYN LEAH

One of the Henschel 0-8-0Ts imported by Peter Court from Mozambique was No. 14968 of 1917, Sena Sugar Estates No. 15, which was restored by Nigel Heath and ran briefly on the North Gloucestershire Railway in 2013-14 before he sold it on to a Belgian zoo. It is seen in action at Toddington during the Cotswold Festival of Steam on May 25, 2014. ROBIN JONES

BRITAIN'S ONLY KRIEGSLOK

One of the predominant locomotive types produced in Nazi Germany was the Deutsche Reichsbahn Class 52 Kriegslok, of which around 6300 were built for use on the Eastern Front, some using forced labour at Polish factories in occupied Poznan and Chrzanów.

Mirroring the USATC S160 2-8-0s and the British War Department Austerity locomotives, Class 52 was a wartime development of the prewar Class 50, using fewer parts and less expensive materials to speed production during wartime shortages. The no-nonsense 2-10-0s were built to a basic, raw and starkly brutal design with few refinements; huge smoke deflectors being their most prominent feature.

Reichsbahn Oberrat Richard Wagner, chief of design in the design office of the Deutsche Reichsbahn from 1922-42 came up with the blueprint for them.

He wanted locomotives that were long-lasting and easy to maintain, and unlike British engineers did not consider high power-to-weight ratio a priority. The Class 52s had a low axleload of 15 tons and could haul 40% more freight than the Prussian locomotives they replaced. They could haul 4000 tons at 50mph without significant strain.

Wagner, incidentally, in 1936, was given a gold medal of service by the Society of British Locomotive Engineers. He is well remembered for the standard smoke deflectors on Deutsche Reichsbahn locomotives, a type adopted by British Railways for A3 Pacifics in the Fifties as evidenced by No. 60103 *Flying Scotsman* today.

To build the vast number of Class 52s, the German locomotive manufacturers were merged into the Gemeinschaft Grossdeutscher Lokomotivhersteller, which came under Reichsminister for munition and armament, Albert Speer and the Reich

transport minister, Julius Dorpmüller.

The Class 52s emerged during Operation Reinhard which was the mass deportation of Jews and other races hated by the Nazis to death camps, and it is likely that the Kriegsloks were used to haul trains for this purpose.

After the war, Class 52s continued to be built, and it is estimated that a total of 6719 appeared, making it one of the biggest classes of locomotive of all time anywhere in the world.

War-torn Europe did not care about who had built the 52s or for what purpose, and eagerly gave them a new lease of life on the railways of liberated countries. The USSR had more than 2100, Poland more than 1200 and East Germany had around 800. Others were to be found in Norway, Romania, Hungary, Czechoslovakia and Turkey. The last in regular main line service were in Austria, which withdrew them in 1976.

Several have been preserved, including one at the Franconian Museum Railway

in Bavaria, and another in the Norwegian Railway Museum.

One of them has run in Britain, on the Nene Valley Railway, which is unique among UK heritage lines in that it can accept stock built to the wider continental Berne loading gauge.

Built in Floridsdorf in Austria in for the war effort as No. 52-7173, it entered service on the Eastern Front between Poland and Russia.

From October 1950 it was reallocated to Russia's South Western Railway, and in October 1957 moved to the Odessa Railway. In April 1962 it went to the Byelorussian Railway and subsequently transferred to Poland in 1963. Class 52s were classified as Ty2 by state railway operator PKP and it was allocated the number Ty2-7173. Its final duty was heavy sand traffic in block trains in the south of Poland near Katowice.

In 1989, British enthusiast, Martin Haines, bought it from PKP on condition it had a full overhaul, so the following year it

Kriegslok 2-10-0 Ty2-713 passes Castor with a Nene Valley Railway Santa special on December 15, 1991. BRIAN SHARPE

went to Olesnica Works and was completely stripped down and rebuilt before being shipped to Britain.

It arrived at the Nene Valley's Wansford base from Felixstowe Docks by road on December 20, 1990. A steam test took place the following month after modification to the trackwork under Lynch Farm Bridge to accommodate it.

During 1992, Ty2-7173 changed identities to that of a German locomotive as Class 52 No. 52-713.

It was withdrawn from service in 2001 and later sold to Patrimoine Ferroviaire et Tourisme, a museum collection in Belgium. Since 2013, it has been cosmetically restored as Belgian Class 26 No. 26.102.

Built in 1944 for the German military by Societe Franco-Belge in occupied France to a design by Berliner Maschinenbau AG (Schwartzkopff), the locomotive was intended to support the German army on the Eastern Front.

However, it is believed that it did not see service before the German rail stores depot fell to Allied occupation forces, and instead it passed in 1946 to the Salzkammergut-Lokalbahn near Salzburg in Austria.

The loco spent 23 years on the Austrian narrow gauge, during which time it was sold to the Steiermärkische Landesbahnen (StLB)

The only Class 52 Kriegslok ever to have run in Britain stands outside Wansford shed. HUGH LLEWELLYN

in 1955. Here it received its 699.01 number and was rebuilt from an 0-8-0 side tank and tender configuration to become a purely side tank engine. It operated freight trains on the StLB's Feistritztalbahn branch line until 1965 when it was

withdrawn from service and stored.

Soon after the WLLR formed strong links with the Austrian lines, which were of the same gauge, and the result was the arrival in Wales of the first of the signature Austrian balcony-ended carriages in 1968.

DESTINED FOR THE EASTERN FRONT – BUT STOPPED IN ITS TRACKS!

Another locomotive built for the Nazi war effort is to be found on the Welshpool & Llanfair Light Railway, but it is not believed to have taken part in any military operations.

No. 699.01 *Sir Drefaldwyn*, the heritage line's No. 10, was built in 1944 for the German military by Société Franco-Belge in occupied France to a design by Berliner Maschinenbau AG (Schwartzkopff).

It was intended to support the German army on the Eastern Front, but it's believed that the engine did not see service before the German rail stores depot fell to Allied occupation forces, and instead it passed in 1946 to the 2ft 6in gauge Salzkammergut Lokalbahn near Salzburg in Austria and worked for several years on the picturesque Salzburg-Bad Ischl line.

The loco spent 23 years on the Austrian narrow gauge, during which time it was sold to the Steiermärkische Landesbahnen in 1955. There it received its 699.01 number and was

rebuilt from an 0-8-0 side tank and tender configuration to become a purely side tank engine. It operated freight trains on the StLB's Feistritztalbahn branch line until 1965 when it was withdrawn from service and stored.

Soon after the Welshpool & Llanfair formed strong links with the Austrian lines, which were of the same gauge, a set of Austrian balcony-ended carriages from the Zillertalbahn including one from the Salzkammergut Lokalbahn arrived in 1968.

The heritage line badly needed another locomotive, and the same Austrian links revealed No. 699.01. An inspection showed that it was in basically good condition, and, with members donating the £1200 cost, it arrived in Llanfair Caereinion on December 11, 1969.

Named *Sir Drefaldwyn* – the Welsh name for Montgomeryshire – entered service on the railway in May 1970.

Welshpool and Llanfair Light Railway No. 10 *Sir Drefaldwyn* at Llanfair Caereinion in October 1990. HEC TATE*

Over the next two decades *Sir Drefaldwyn* proved a stalwart member of the fleet, particularly renowned for its heavy-hauling capability. However, at the end of the 1990s major boiler repairs became necessary and it was withdrawn when its boiler ticket expired on May 7, 2000; it was then placed on static display.

In 2014, an appeal was launched to overhaul *Sir Drefaldwyn*, the cost of which was estimated to be around £62,000.

In spring 2015, the overhaul of the boiler at the Severn Valley Railway's Bridgnorth Works was completed and it returned to Llanfair Caereinion, where volunteers aim to have their No. 10 steaming through the Banwy valley again in late 2016 or early 2017.

So, a locomotive that was ordered to be built for use by Nazi war-mongers spent its life serving purely peaceful purposes, and is now looking to a bright future of doing much of the same.

Franco-Belge 0-8-0T No. 699.01 *Sir Drefaldwyn* heads the Welshpool & Llanfair Light Railway's rake of Austrian coaches into Llanfair Caereinion station in spring 1971. ROBIN JONES

Rail history at your fingertips!

WHAT'S IT ALL ABOUT?

You told us that you wanted to access *The Railway Magazine's* archive online. Well now you can.

We listened to our readers... and we have acted... and right now we'd like to give you the chance to gain access to our superb online archive!

The Railway Magazine's history stretches back to the late 19th century, and we now have 60 years' worth of content already scanned with new issues being added daily. By the end of 2016, the entire Archive will be live!

Complete searchable back issues of Britain's best-selling rail title already online include those from the early part of this millennium, some from key years in the 20th century, as well as many fascinating issues from when the very first edition of *The Railway Magazine* was published in 1897.

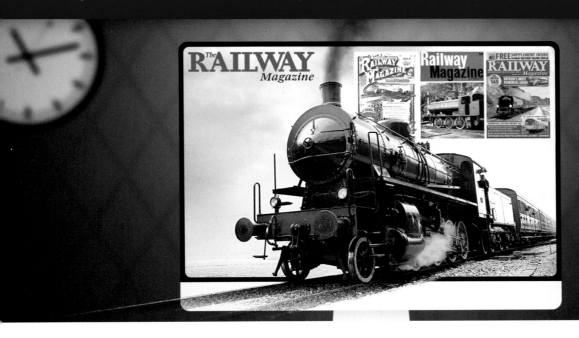

WHAT DOES IT COST?

We have invested heavily in some new technology to make this possible, and our team is busy scanning in many decades'-worth of content to give you the most comprehensive railways archive anywhere in the world. So we hope you agree that an average cost of just **£1 per month** for this represents superb value for money.

SIGN ME UP!

CURRENT SUBSCRIBERS

To add access to the Archive on to your current subscription, go to classicmagazines.co.uk/rmarchive and click on the 'My Account' button at the top. You'll need your Customer ID, surname and postcode to login, then you'll be well away.

NOT A SUBSCRIBER?

At present, Archive access is only available to subscribers of *The Railway Magazine*. To get started visit classicmagaines.co.uk/trm63 and search *The Railway Magazine*, or give our team a call on 01507 529529.

FOR MORE INFORMATION VISIT: classicmagazines.co.uk/rmarchive

The RAILWAY *Magazine*

VICTORS
in steam

Two British Pacific locomotives were saved from the scrapman at the end of steam in the Sixties, purely because of their illustrious names; Sir Winston Churchill and Dwight D. Eisenhower, and both have in recent times starred in showpiece events at the National Railway Museum.

AT 8am on Friday, January 30, 2015 a whistle was sounded as a train was shunted into the National Railway Museum at York to choral accompaniment.

As a crowd of VIPs from across Britain fell silent, Bulleid Battle of Britain Pacific No. 34051 *Winston Churchill* – which had undergone a stunning cosmetic refurbishment at the Mid Hants Railway's Ropley Works – entered the Great Hall in front of a rake of two vehicles, which had also formed part of

the great wartime leader's state funeral train exactly 50 years before.

Firstly there was the humble Southern Railway parcels van No. S2464S, in which, during restoration, the markings for the resting place of the coffin of the wartime prime minister had been rediscovered.

Then came Pullman car No. 246 *Lydia*, which had, during the Second World War, formed part of Churchill's command train.

The entry of the re-created funeral

train kicked off a series of nationwide commemorative events with a flotilla down the Thames including the barge that had carried Churchill's coffin in 1965, alongside the stretch where, famously, the dockyard cranes bowed their jibs in respect as it passed by.

As with the train that carried the coffin and world leaders from Waterloo to Handborough station in Oxfordshire, the three headcode discs on No. 34051 were

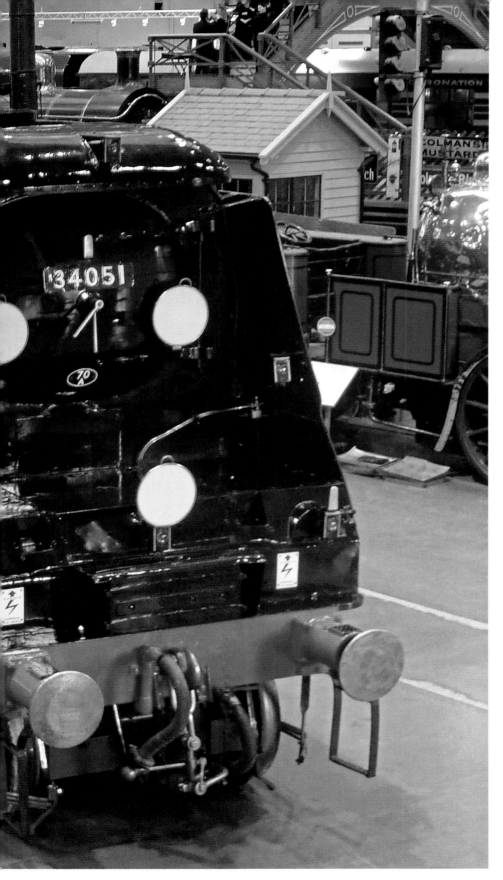

LEFT: Carrying a headcode mirroring Churchill's V for Victory salute, No. 34051 *Sir Winston Churchill* stands at the head of the re-created funeral train after making a triumphant entry into the National Railway Museum's Great Hall to the accompaniment of a chamber choir on January 30, 2015, half a century to the day after the great wartime prime minister's funeral. ROBIN JONES

An accompanying display included archive news footage of the funeral, which saw the crowds throng the lineside throughout Churchill's final journey, as men doffed their caps and hats before bowing their heads in respect as the rake of Pullman carriages flashed by in a cloud of smoke and steam, while 300 million more worldwide clustered around their TV sets to bid farewell to the hero who had saved Europe.

However, the star of the show this time round was Jim Lester, 72, the fireman on the footplate of No. 34051 on that historic journey half a century before.

He said: "It's been great working with the museum on this display to mark this anniversary and for me; it's like turning the clock back 50 years. I'm a little more hard of hearing than I was back then but the sound of that whistle and seeing the locomotive and train, together again, has brought it all back to me, the huge crowds watching us go past and the deep sense of sadness that was evident on the occasion."

Also present was Steve Davies, the former museum director who during his tenure had asked for No. 34051 to be restored because of its deteriorating condition.

No. 34051 was withdrawn on September 19, 1965, and because of its name it was earmarked for preservation and joined the National Collection in 1966. It had been on static display throughout its decades as a popular exhibit in the museum.

Anthony Coulls, the museum's senior curator of rail vehicles, said: "Our locomotive and the carriages that it hauled have earned a place on the national stage thanks to the part they played in Churchill's final journey. Until they were chosen to take the statesman on his final farewell, they were just standard rolling stock, especially the baggage van."

Also given pride of place on the occasion was the team from Ropley Works, which carried out the meticulous restoration of No. 34051, after it had been found that not only had the paintwork faded but much of the trademark 'Spam can' casing had rotted away from the inside. Also in attendance were their counterparts from the Locomotion museum in Shildon who had restored the baggage car.

Elsewhere, Britain's three main party leaders, none of whom were born when the nation turned out in vast numbers to mourn Churchill's death, laid wreaths at his Commons statue. Winston's great-great grandchildren, Iona Pite, John Winston Churchill and Christabel Fraser, laid a wreath during a commemoration at Westminster Abbey.

arranged in a unique V formation, recalling Churchill's famous Victory sign.

On January 30, 1965, the most famous Pullman train of all time had comprised six coaches carrying the coffin and mourners from Waterloo station to Churchill's final resting place, following his death at the age of 91, and funeral service in St Paul's cathedral.

From Handborough station, the coffin was taken by road to St Martin's church in the village of Bladon near Churchill's family's ancestral seat of Blenheim Palace in Oxfordshire.

The re-created funeral train remained on display in the Great Hall until May 3, 2015 at the centrepiece of an exhibition that recalled the part the railway played in the only state funeral granted to a statesman in the 20th century. It was also the last steam-hauled state funeral to be held in Britain.

CHURCHILL PULLMAN CARS COME HOME

No. 246 *Lydia* was one of two 1925-built Pullman cars from the 1965 funeral train that ended up in exile for 31 years in the USA, until they were repatriated in the autumn of 2000.

It was in gale-force conditions and torrential rain that *Lydia* and No. 246 *Isle of Thanet* were craned off the transatlantic cargo vessel *Stella Nova* at Newport Docks on November 11 that year.

They had been bought for an undisclosed sum by enthusiast David Westcott, who supports the Swanage Railway, to be used as part of a new first-class 'Wessex Belle' dining train on its line in the Isle of Purbeck.

After they were unloaded from the ship, the coaches were whisked away on the back of low loaders to Carnforth near the Lake District, where they were expertly restored to as-new condition by the West Coast Railway Company. Apart from *Lydia's* appearance on the re-created museum train, they have remained in secure store ever since, until such time as the Swanage Railway is able to provide adequate undercover accommodation.

The two coaches had been bought from British Railways by the US National Railroad Museum at Green Bay in Wisconsin, along with another pair of carriages, which had formed part of General Eisenhower's British wartime command train.

When the world's most famous steam locomotive, Gresley A3 Pacific No. 4472 *Flying Scotsman*, embarked on a tour of North America in 1969, it was arranged that the two

Pullmans could form part of its train provided that they were delivered to the museum.

One of the coaches was delivered as planned – but the tour and the locomotive's owner Alan Pegler later went bankrupt, leaving *Flying Scotsman* and the rest of its train stranded in California.

The destitute Alan Pegler had to work his passage home to Britain as a ship's entertainer, while money had to then be raised by the US museum to move its second Pullman across the States to Green Bay eventually.

The pair were repatriated after months of secret negotiations with the museum by Swanage Railway officials on behalf of a buyer. The coaches were found to be a living time capsule – with the dining cards from the ill-fated *Flying Scotsman* tour 30 years before still on the tables inside!

After the 800-mile journey from Green Bay to Montreal in Canada, the two coaches were loaded on to the *Stella Nova* – belonging to the Dutch Jumbo shipping line – on Monday, October 23, 2000 for the 3500-mile voyage to Newport. The ship sailed for Britain on October 28. But a snowstorm in the St Lawrence River meant that it had to take shelter before continuing its transatlantic journey.

Also on board the ship was a consignment of eight brand new Class 66 diesel-electric locomotives, built by General Motors at its factory in London, Canada, for service with Freightliner in Britain.

Pullman carriage *Lydia* was manufactured by the Birmingham Carriage & Wagon Company in 1925. It was significantly damaged when it was struck by an excursion train just outside Leeds Central station in 1959, but was repaired at Preston Park works for a grand total of £820. The Pullman Society provided interior table lamps for the funeral train exhibition.
ROBIN JONES

AND MORE WERE TO FOLLOW

It appeared that the Swanage Railway had been bitten by the repatriation bug.

The railway is also home to Drummond LSWR M7 0-4-4T No. 30053, which was repatriated to Britain from Pennsylvania's Steamtown Museum under the leadership of the late Trevor Heard. The one-time Bournemouth engine made its first run on the Purbeck Line on June 6, 1992, five years after it was returned to Britain and restored at Swindon and the East Anglian Railway Museum.

Officials of the Purbeck line successfully negotiated a deal to bring back 'Devon Belle' Pullman observation car No. 14 – another of the coaches left stranded in

California by the failure of the *Flying Scotsman* tour – home at last, thanks to financial assistance from Bodmin & Wenford Railway benefactor, Alan Moore, who offered to fund half the cost of the repatriation.

Proud Swanage Railway Trust officials watched as Car 14 was unloaded from the 66,532-ton Wallenius Wilhelmsen Logistics roll-on, roll-off ship *MV Taiko* at Southampton Docks on Monday, February 26, 2007, before it was taken away by low loader to Ramparts of Derby where it was restored to serviceable condition.

Swanage attention then turned to a third vehicle from Churchill's funeral train, the Parcels Luggage Van that had carried his coffin.

No. S2464S had ended up on display

at the City of Industry golf course near Los Angeles, and had been offered free to the heritage line. An appeal for funds to repatriate the van was successfully launched.

On October 2, 2007, the 1931-built van arrived at Southampton Docks on Wallenius Wilhelmsen Logistics' vessel *Tamerlane* at the end of a six-week 8000-mile journey home via the Panama Canal. Los Angeles Mayor David Perez had offered it as "a gift to the British people" and previous owner, the City of Industry, sponsored the transportation costs.

From there it was taken to the East Somerset Railway's carriage depot at Cranmore where a full assessment of its condition was carried out.

The van had been specially repainted

No. 34051 at the head of the funeral train on January 30, 1965, MIKE EVANS

RIGHT: On January 30, from the footplate of No. 34051, National Railway Museum director Paul Kirkman officially opens the funeral train exhibition watched by Philip Benham, chairman of the museum's Friends group. ROBIN JONES

LEFT: Jim Lester, the fireman on the funeral train 50 years previously, is reunited with *Winston Churchill*. Built at Brighton Works in 1946 as No. 21C151, the locomotive was released to traffic on December 30 that year, and was first allocated to Salisbury shed for services between London and Exeter. It was officially named *Winston Churchill* in a ceremony at Waterloo on September 11, 1947. In October 1948 it received its British Railways' number, 34051. ROBIN JONES

in Pullman colours three years before Churchill died, in anticipation of its eventual role.

Later in 1965, the van was saved from being scrapped and was exported to California thanks to the late Darius Johnson of the City of Industry. It was subsequently placed on display at a resort hotel near Los Angeles.

The Swanage Railway, which used the baggage car as a store since it was repatriated, agreed to allow it to be cosmetically restored at the Locomotion museum in Shildon for the planned exhibition to mark the 50th anniversary of the funeral.

The restorations of both No. 34051 and the van were supported by the Friends of the National Railway Museum, which had launched an appeal back in January 2011, to raise funds for the project.

Staff, volunteers and trainees at Locomotion finished the comprehensive structural work required to bring the van back to its former glory in late November 2014.

Anthony Coulls said: "Until it was chosen to carry the great man's coffin 50 years ago, this was just a regular goods van carrying things like vegetables and newspapers."

ABOVE LEFT: Southern Railway Parcels Luggage Van No. S2464S reprised its role in Sir Winston Churchill's funeral train 50 years on. ROBIN JONES
LEFT: The interior of No. S2464S, where Churchill's coffin was carried on its final journey. ROBIN JONES

BACK ON DISPLAY

During 2016, No. 34051 and the parcels van went on display at Locomotion, again to commemorate the state funeral.

Interpretation panels and newsreel footage showing the impact that Sir Winston Churchill's final journey had on the nation completed the display, which was scheduled to run until late in the year.

Locomotion's learning team offers a schools package for Key Stage 2 children, which links to Sir Winston Churchill and explores what life was like for youngsters evacuated during the Second World War.

Bulleid Battle of Britain Pacific No. 34051 *Winston Churchill* inside Locomotion. LOCOMOTION

Sir Winston Churchill and Dwight D. Eisenhower.

GWR COACH FIT FOR WORLD LEADERS

BUCKINGHAMSHIRE Railway Centre is the location of another carriage with links to great wartime leaders.

GWR Special Saloon No. W9001 was built in 1940 to diagram G62, lot No. 1626 and used by Churchill when entertaining General Dwight D. Eisenhower, Supreme Commander of the Allied Forces in Europe.

It was – and still is – equipped with a lounge, dining room, kitchen and pantry.

No. W90001 entered preservation in 1968 on the Severn Valley Railway. In 1976 it moved to the Birmingham Railway Museum at Tyseley, and was then loaned to the Great Central Railway, before being returned to Tyseley.

In early 2002, it was loaned to the centre at Quainton Road for display in the new Rewley Road visitor centre, and was sold to the venue in 2007.

The carriage was sent for fast-track restoration to the Llangollen Railway, returning to Quainton Road in December 2007. Some internal work was completed there during 2008.

Visitors can enter the coach and see many of the fittings that would have been there during the meetings between the two leaders – a true Second World War timewarp in deepest Buckinghamshire!

RIGHT: The compartment inside No. W9001 in which the two great wartime leaders met. ROBIN JONES

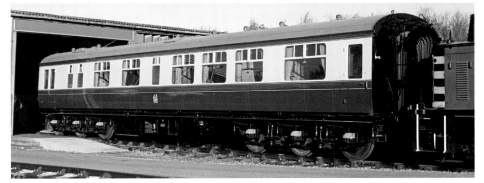

GWR Special Saloon No. W9001 in which Sir Winston Churchill entertained future US president Dwight D. Eisenhower. ANDREW BRATTON

A4 Pacific No. 60008 *Dwight D. Eisenhower* is lifted aboard the United States Lines SS *American Planter* at Southampton Docks on April 2, 1964, after being handed over by British Railways chairman Dr Richard Beeching, a name synonymous with the mass closures of unprofitable railway lines during the demise of steam haulage in the 1960s. THE RAILWAY MAGAZINE

World steam railway speed record holder *Mallard* was also cosmetically restored for the Great Gathering. Then National Railway Museum director, Steve Davies, who had set up the Great Gathering, took the opportunity to parade No. 4468 in black undercoat, very similar to the wartime black livery carried by all members of the class in the early Forties to reduce maintenance costs. ROBIN JONES

MISSION IMPOSSIBLE ACCOMPLISHED

Over the years, there had been several attempts by people involved in the UK heritage sector to repatriate both No. 60008 and sister No. 60010 *Dominion of Canada*, which, by virtue of its name, had also been saved, and given to the Exporail museum at Montreal. In all cases, such requests were rebuffed by both museums.

However, in August 2011, a world exclusive by *Heritage Railway* magazine revealed that National Railway Museum director Steve Davies had pulled off the impossible. Both museums would allow their A4s to come home to join in celebrations to mark the centenary of *Mallard's* record run in exchange for having them cosmetically restored.

Locomotive repatriation expert, Andrew

HONOURING IKE TOO

Sir Winston Churchill was not the only world leader to have a British locomotive named in his honour following the Allies' victory in the Second World War.

When it entered traffic on September 4, 1937, LNER A4 streamlined Pacific No. 4496 was named *Golden Shuttle* and painted in LNER garter blue with stainless-steel trim on the base of the valances and tender. The numbers and LNER lettering on the tender were also stainless steel, and it had a single chimney and side valances covering the wheels.

This livery design was also used on the A4s that were named after countries, on the 'Coronation' service in order to match the rolling stock. This locomotive was originally to have been named Sparrow Hawk, but that name was later used on No. 4463.

It was painted wartime black on January 30, 1942, when the valances were removed, with the livery modified on March 12, 1943, the tender lettering reduced to NE.

On September 25, 1945, the garter blue livery was reapplied, and the name changed to that of Dwight D. Eisenhower, the Supreme Commander of Allied Forces during the latter part of the Second World War – breaking the tradition of renaming engines after LNER officials.

The name was covered up until February 1946. It was intended that Eisenhower himself would attend an official unveiling, but it could not be arranged. It was also renumbered 8 on November 23, 1946.

After Nationalisation it became No. 60008 on October 29, 1948. British Railways' dark-blue livery with black and white lining was applied on June 14, 1950 and Brunswick green on November 9, 1951.

Golden Shuttle, which was allocated to work the 'West Riding Limited', was first allocated to Doncaster, during September 20-29, 1937. Then it was moved to King's Cross until December 4, 1939 when it was reallocated to Grantham. On June 4, 1950, it went back to King's Cross.

Another move to Grantham came on April 7, 1957, with it again returning to King's Cross, on September 15, 1957. Its final allocation was New England shed in Peterborough from June 16, 1963, four days before it was withdrawn from service, and it appeared to all that the scrapman was waiting.

However, in the Fifties, as steam disappeared from US railroads earlier than in Britain, a National Railroad Museum was established at Green Bay. A chance conversation between a Mrs Kovachek, who was holidaying from Yorkshire, and a man she thought was the museum's gardener, resulted in No. 60008 ending up in the USA.

The 'gardener' turned out to be the chairman of the museum's board, Harold E Fuller. When he found out that there was a locomotive named *Dwight D. Eisenhower* in the UK, he became determined to add it to the collection. British Railways, however, would not sell it to him.

General Eisenhower had strong connections with Britain's railways, as there had been two military command trains in Britain during the run-up to D-Day, which were for the future president's exclusive use. These trains, mainly of GWR stock and codenamed Alive, included two LNER Gresley coaches, which were the general's favourites.

After No. 60008 was withdrawn, BR was happy to donate the engine and the two LNER coaches used by the General to the Green Bay museum.

Still in BR green livery, as cosmetically restored at Doncaster Works on July 19, 1963 before its export across the Atlantic, it was shipped to the US, arriving in New York Harbour on May 11, 1964. It was taken by rail to the museum later that month, and was displayed with the coaches for many years from 1964.

In October 1990 it was moved to Abilene, Kansas for the celebrations of the centenary of Eisenhower's birth. The move both ways was carried out as a special train at slow speed, since the locomotive and two cars from the command train used the British vacuum braking system, which is incompatible with US air-braked trains.

In 2000, *Dwight D. Eisenhower* was given pride of place in a new museum building at Green Bay, still with the Gresley coaches attached, and standing alongside Union Pacific articulated 4-8-8-4 'Big-Boy' No. 4017, the idea being that a member of the world's fastest class of steam locomotive – sister A4 No. 4468 *Mallard* hit 126mph on Stoke Bank in Lincolnshire on July 3, 1938 – stands next to the world's biggest.

It was only in recent times that research on both sides of the Atlantic led its US custodians to realise that No. 60008 would almost certainly never have hauled either of its namesake's military trains in Britain during the Second World War.

No. 60008 (second left) in place around the turntable in the National Railway Museum's Great Hall for the Autumn Great Gathering of all six surviving A4s in 2013. ROBIN JONES

Goodman, of Moveright International sponsored and handled the incredibly complicated transportation of the pair across North America to the port of Halifax, including the extraction of *Dwight D. Eisenhower* from the museum shed into which it had been effectively bricked into, by moving it sideways on a bespoke sled.

On October 3, 2012 Nos. 60008 and 60010 arrived at Liverpool, and were then taken by road to the Locomotion museum.

The cosmetic restoration of No. 60008 was completed in February 2013 and it was displayed in the Great Hall at York next to illustrious sister No. 4498 *Mallard.*

No. 60008 was joined by the five surviving members of the class at the Great Gathering; *Mallard*, No. 60007 *Sir Nigel Gresley*, No. 60009 *Union of South Africa*, No. 4464 *Bittern*, and *Dominion of Canada*, cosmetically restored with valances as No. 4489.

The first of three Mallard 75 reunions were held at the museum from July 3. A second gathering was staged there in the autumn, and the final event featuring all six A4s was the Great Goodbye at Locomotion in February 2014.

Mallard 75 was one of the most spectacular and poignant moments in the history of railway preservation. Nearly three years of planning had finally come to fruition, to honour Britain's record-holder.

During this time, the Green Bay museum was offered $1 million by a private buyer in Berkshire to have the engine remain in Britain for restoration to main line order, and he even sent a cheque for that amount in the post. As always, the offer was rejected.

Both expatriate A4s reached Halifax on May 11, 2014, and were transferred on to flat cars to be taken by rail to their museum homes. No. 60008 arrived at Green Bay on June 6, 2014. The museum officially unveiled the engine as part of a new Second World War-themed exhibition on August 2, 2014.

Green Bay museum executive director, Jacqueline Frank, proudly stands alongside *Dwight D. Eisenhower* at the start of the Great Gathering at York on July 3, 2013. ROBIN JONES

Dwight D. Eisenhower back on British soil at Liverpool Docks on October 3, 2012. ROBIN JONES

No. 60008 *Dwight D. Eisenhower* in the National Railway Museum in February 2013, having just been cosmetically restored. ROBIN JONES

Island at WAR

It is not only on mainland Britain that heritage railways commemorate the Second World War with re-enactments. The Isle of Man Steam Railway now holds a rip-roaring Forties weekend each summer.

Beyer Peacock 2-4-0T No. 10 GH Wood heads an Isle of Man Steam Railway service past a crashed Spitfire. IOMR

Home produce for the Home Front! IOMR

The Fabulous D-Day Darlings sing in three-part harmony at various stations along with local Forties singers and choirs. IOMR

During the Second World War, the Germans, who laid their own narrow gauge systems supplementing those already in existence, occupied the Chanel Islands. However, the Crown dependency of the Isle of Man, well away from the front line of German attacks in the middle of the Irish Sea, was also hit by an invasion of foreigners from Europe, but in a very different way.

It found itself, in both world wars, used for internment camps, mainly for civilian nationals belonging to countries on the opposing side.

At the start of the Second World War, there were around 80,000 potential enemy aliens in Britain who could be spies, or willing to assist Britain's enemies in the event of an invasion, it was feared, often with some degree of paranoia. For instance, when Italy and Britain declared hostilities, there were at least 19,000 Italians in Britain, and Churchill ordered that all were rounded up and interned – despite the fact that most of them had lived in Britain for several decades.

Thousands of Germans, Austrians and Italians were sent to camps set up at racecourses and incomplete housing estates, such as Huyton outside Liverpool. The majority were interned on the Isle of Man.

In one Isle of Man camp more than 80% of the internees were Jewish refugees.

That many of the 'enemy aliens' were Jewish refugees and therefore hardly likely to be sympathetic to the Nazis, was a complication no one bothered to try and unravel – they were still treated as German and Austrian nationals.

An outcry in Parliament led to the first releases of internees in August 1940, and by February 1941 more than 10,000 had been freed. By summer 1942, only 5000 were left in internment camps.

The island was, and still is, famous for its network of 3ft gauge railways. During the Second World War, the usual winter timetable of seven or eight trains per day each way on all three main routes, from Douglas to Port Erin, Peel and Ramsey between 7am and 8pm ran throughout.

However, as the number of servicemen on the island increased because of military defensive requirements it became the custom to run additional late trains on Fridays and Saturdays. Special military trains being run, often very early in the morning.

Passenger services on the Foxdale branch ceased in 1940, but it became heavily used for spoil trains during the construction of Jurby and Ronaldsway aerodromes.

Since 2011, the Isle of Man Steam Railway has commemorated the dark days with an annual Island at War event.

Castletown station becomes the main wartime hub with Explorer Scouts and cadets providing a military presence and

A re-creation of an internees' assembly point. IOMR

Typical Forties characters re-created for the annual Island at War event. IOMR

a field hospital. Local hairdressers stage a 'hair-raid shelter' in a vintage bus creating quick wartime styles while passengers wait for the train, while there are also period vehicles from the Isle of Man Motor Museum and elsewhere.

Port Erin enters into the spirit of the 'home front' with all the shops dressed accordingly. The Whistle Stop transforms into René's cafe and Women's Institute stalls offer homemade cakes and jams, an exhibition and presentation about internees and a Morse code interactive display.

For the 2016 event, scheduled for August 19-21 the Manx Electric Railway and Snaefell Mountain Railway are to take part in the event.

Timetabled events evoking the sights and sounds of the Second World War will include a 'crashed' Spitfire at Snaefell summit and an artillery vehicle guarded by cadets.

Anji Street, IoM Railways' events co-ordinator, said: "It's going from strength to strength. We couldn't do it without the enthusiastic support of many groups and individuals, which we are hugely grateful for, and we look forward to hordes of residents and visitors dressing up and participating over the weekend.

"An integral element is to commemorate the part local servicemen played in the war."

* More details can be found at www.rail.im

A tank stands sentinel as an Isle of Man Steam Railway service passes. IOMR

The new National Memorial Engine

Many events have taken place at heritage railway venues to mark the centenary of key dates from the First World War. However, the greatest of them awaits in 2018, when to mark 100 years since the Armistice, a new monument will be unveiled.

Endorsed by the Royal British Legion, No. 45551 *The Unknown Warrior* is an all-new LMS Patriot 4-6-0, which will become the National Memorial Engine, honouring Britain's servicemen and women who died in both world wars and subsequent conflicts – a steam 'version' of the Cenotaph.

After the First World War, three railway companies named locomotives to honour employees who had fought and died during the conflict.

The Great Central Railway named 9P (LNER B3) 4-6-0 1165 *Valour*. The name is now carried by GB Railfreight Class 66 No. 66715 *Valour*.

The LBSCR named L class 4-6-4T No. 333 *Remembrance*.

The LNWR named Claughton class 4-6-0 No. 1914 *Patriot*. The name was later removed and used on LMS Patriot 4-6-0 No. (4)5500. It became the new 'Patriot' memorial engine for the LMS, after which the entire class took the name.

Plans are now well advanced to build a new LMS Patriot, none of which survived the end of steam. The locomotive will be a memorial not just to the fallen of both world wars, but to servicemen and women who gave their lives in subsequent conflicts, and is therefore just as relevant today as it would have been a century ago.

Being built by the LMS-Patriot Project at an estimated cost of £1.5 million, the new locomotive, which is now a rolling chassis, has received the endorsement of The Royal British Legion. Numbered 45551, the next in the series, it will carry a Legion crest above *The Unknown Warrior* nameplate.

No. 45551 is being built for main line running, and judging by the crowds turning out to see £3-million new-build A1 Peppercorn Pacific No. 60163 *Tornado* wherever it goes, it will be a huge attraction on the railway network.

It is aimed to have No. 45551 ready to run by November 11, 1918, the centenary of

In late 2013, Colin Wright produced an oil painting of new-build LMS Patriot 4-6-0 No. 45551 *The Unknown Warrior* to mark its first public appearances away from its Llangollen construction base, and to raise more funds for its completion. It depicts No. 45551 in pre-1936 LMS crimson lake livery outside Crewe North Shed with the original LNWR Memorial Engine: Claughton Patriot No. 5964, in May 1934, when the original No. 5551 had just been outshopped. The Claughton Patriot lasted only another two months before withdrawal in July 1934. The trio of locomotives outside the shed is completed by the last 'Large Jumbo', No. 25001 *Snowdon*. In the background lurks George the Fifth 4-4-0 No. 5401 *Windermere*. LMS-PATRIOT PROJECT

~COLIN WRIGHT~

Patriot 4-6-0 No. 45519 *Lady Godiva* passes Dore & Totley in June 1960. PJ HUGHES/COLOUR-RAIL

HISTORY OF THE PATRIOTS

The three-cylinder LMS Patriot class was introduced towards the end of Sir Henry Fowler's reign as Chief Mechanical Engineer from 1925-32.

The class was presented as a rebuild of Bowen-Cook's large-boilered Claughton 4-6-0s; indeed, the first two were produced from the remains of two Claughtons that had been badly damaged in accidents, retaining the original driving wheels with their large bosses, the 'double radial' bogie truck and various other parts.

The subsequent 50 locomotives of the Class 40 were nominal rebuilds of Claughtons, being in fact new builds classified as rebuilt engines so that they could be charged to revenue accounts, rather than capital. The last 10 were classified as new builds.

The Patriots, as they were known after 1937, had more in common with the Royal Scot, having a very similar chassis combined with the smaller G91/2S boiler as used on the rebuilt large Claughtons. They were known as 'Baby Scots' as a result.

A total of 57 were planned, but the last five were built with taper boilers and became the first of the Jubilee class.

Between 1946 and 1948, 18 Patriots were rebuilt with Stanier 2A boiler, cab and tender. From 1948 onwards, these were fitted with Royal Scot pattern deflectors. The two original members of the class, and the first 10 of the nominal rebuilds, were not rebuilt owing to their non-standard parts.

All the Patriots were painted out in LMS crimson lake livery with pale yellow and black lining when first built, but after 1946 most were painted out in LMS lined black with straw and maroon lining. All of them were later reliveried in British Railways' standard Brunswick green with orange and black.

Highly successful, the Patriots covered around 1.3 million miles each. They were all withdrawn in 1960-65 and scrapped. The last two to be withdrawn were Nos. 45543 and 45550 *Patriot*, which sadly, was not thought worthy of preservation, despite its heritage.

the Armistice, which ended the First World War.

The project is the brainchild of David Bradshaw, a leading member of the Great Western Society, which has several new-build locomotive projects underway.

David grew up in Midland territory, and saw that the LMS was, in comparison with the Southern and GWR, poorly represented in preservation. In 2006, he came up with the idea of re-creating the class, and not only filling a major gap in today's heritage steam fleet, but also creating a locomotive with the capacity to attract public support far beyond the limits of the railway enthusiast sector.

Taking on the mantle of the Great Central Railway's war memorial locomotive is GBRf Class 66, 66715 *Valour – In Memory Of All Railway Employees Who Gave Their Lives For Their Country* – at Tonbridge. DEREK HOSKINGS *

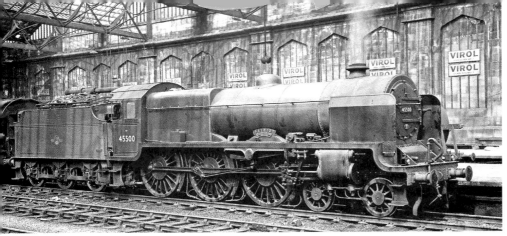

LMS Patriot class 4-6-0 No. 45500 *Patriot* at Carlisle on August 3, 1957. DAVID FORSYTH, COLOUR-RAIL

The LBSCR's war memorial locomotive L class 4-6-4T *Valour*.

THE RALLYING CRY

In July 2007, the scheme to build a new Patriot was floated by David Bradshaw.

The following January, the project received a major boost when LMS Stanier 8F 2-8-0 No. 48518 – one of the last 10 locomotives to be saved from the legendary Barry scrapyard – was taken out of storage at Barry and moved to the Llangollen Railway for its boiler to be lifted, for use on the Great Western Society's new-build Hawksworth County 4-6-0 No. 1014 *County of Glamorgan* at Didcot Railway Centre.

The frames of the 8F, however, remained for use in the recently launched Patriot project, which is seeing the new locomotive built in the Llangollen Railway's workshop.

An appropriate spare Fowler tender also survived from Barry scrapyard, and would be rebuilt for the Patriot with an all-new tender body after being acquired from the Vale of Glamorgan Council.

The project was formally launched at the Llangollen Railway gala on April 18-20, 2008. The event was duly named the Patriot Gala.

A presentation was made to Kevin Finnerty, a resident of Giggleswick, a village near Settle, who came up with the name *The Unknown Warrior*. Coincidentally, one of the Patriots, No. 5538, was named after Giggleswick.

The nameplate of *The Unknown Warrior* with the Royal British Legion crest on top. ROBIN JONES

The North Wales branch of the Royal British Legion unveiled the new Patriot's nameplate design and dedicated the locomotive to the memory of British servicemen. The ceremony was held at the Llangollen Railway's locomotive works on November 2, 2009, nine days before Remembrance Day. Following a dedication speech by Legion representatives delivered in both English and Welsh, a bugler sounded the Last Post before poppy petals rained down on to the frames of No. 45551 and its union-flag draped nameplate. As the Legion standards were dipped, the flag was removed in order to reveal the magnificent new nameplate. In keeping with engineering tradition a bottle was then broken against the frames to confirm the launch of the Patriot project.

In its first few months, the project raised pledges of more than £100,000 towards the estimated total cost of £1.5 million, reflecting the popularity of the type more than 40 years after the last one ran on the national network.

Tyseley Locomotive Works chief engineer, Bob Meanley, offered to loan the set of patterns used to make new driving wheels for Jubilee No. 45699 *Galatea*, which was rebuilt by the West Coast Railway Company at Carnforth and is now a regular performer on the main line.

TAKING SHAPE

Masterminded by Dave Owen, Chief Mechanical Engineer at the Llangollen workshops, the assembly of *The Unknown Warrior* began in 2009.

That March, the frame plates for the new Patriot were cut by Corus Steel at Cradley Heath in the West Midlands. The plates were taken to the Boro' Foundry in nearby Lye for drilling and machining, before being delivered to Llangollen that summer.

It was clear at this early stage that minor adaptations to the original design would have to be made. Running on the national network – which has always been the intention of the project team – would require the locomotive to be built to a height of 13ft; 2½in less than the LMS design. The design of the chimney and cab were affected by the reduced height requirements and additional items that are required for mainline running including

Complete with bogie, *The Unknown Warrior* became a 4-6-0 at Tyseley Locomotive Works for the first time on February 3, 2016. ANDY COLLINSON/LMS-PATRIOT PROJECT

Patriot 4-6-0 No. 45551 *The Unknown Warrior* being shunted by BR Standard 4MT 2-6-4T No. 80072 at Llangollen on March 24, 2016 following its delivery from Tyseley Locomotive Works. It was the first time that the new Patriot had been moved by another steam locomotive. GAVIN SHELL/LMS-PATRIOT PROJECT

Train Protection & Warning System and On-Train Monitoring & Recording apparatus. There was also a possibly air braking also need to be considered.

In January 2011, a set of genuine LMS buffers of the type fitted to Patriots was acquired from a rail-mounted crane that was being scrapped at the Great Central Railway (Nottingham). At least three of the buffers are stamped LMS, with Thirties dates.

THE PUBLIC PAID FOR THE WHEELS

The $60,000 needed for the six driving wheels was raised by readers of *Heritage Railway* magazine though an appeal launched on the front cover of issue 131.

The first driving wheel for *The Unknown Warrior* was cast at Boro' Foundry on September 14, 2010.

It took just 90 seconds for molten steel to be poured into the mould. Two days later the finished wheel was lifted out.

At 6ft 9in, it was believed to be the biggest standard gauge locomotive wheel cast in the heritage era, beating the 6ft 8 ½in wheels for new-build GWR Saint No. 2999 *Lady of Legend* by just half an inch.

All six driving wheels were cast by January 2011. The fitting of the tyres, crank axle, plain axles and crank pins was contracted to the South Devon Railway, which assembled the six new wheelsets in January 2013.

The completed driving wheelsets for new LMS Patriot No. 45551 *The Unknown Warrior* were delivered to Tyseley Locomotive Works at the beginning of July 2013.

At Tyseley they were balanced with lead weights, turned and had the axleboxes fitted before being taken to the Llangollen Railway Works to be fitted to the frames of *The Unknown Warrior* to enable the rolling chassis (minus the front bogie), to be completed.

The rolling chassis with smokebox was displayed at the Warley Model Railway Exhibition that year.

TOP RIGHT: Pouring the metal for the new wheels at Boro' Foundry in Lye. ROBIN JONES

RIGHT: Author Robin Jones with one of the newly cast wheels at Boro' Foundry on September 15, 2010. ROBIN JONES COLLECTION

PETE WATERMAN LAUNCHES BOILER APPEAL

On November 19, 2010, it was announced that LNWR Heritage Ltd at Crewe had been chosen as the preferred builder of the boiler.

The all-new boiler is being built in the traditional way, with a copper firebox, riveted seams and screwed stays.

LNWR Heritage Ltd, then owned by pop mogul Pete Waterman had already built new copper fireboxes at Crewe, including the one for LNER B1 4-6-0 No. 61264 owned by the Thompson B1 Locomotive Trust, and the spare A4 boiler for LNER Pacific No. 60019 *Bittern*.

When completed, the new Patriot boiler will be the first traditionally built large steam boiler to be built in the UK for a standard gauge main line steam locomotive since 1960.

Steve Blackburn, engineering and quality director for the LMS-Patriot Project said, "Crewe is the obvious choice for building the boiler for *The Unknown Warrior*. With LNWR's technical capabilities and the historical links going back to the original Patriots at Crewe, we are delighted that the new boiler will be

constructed in the railway town that was synonymous with the LMS and world-renowned railway engineering."

A national fundraising campaign for the new boiler was launched on May 19, 2012.

The boiler barrel sections for LMS Patriot 4-6-0 No. 45551 *The Unknown Warrior* were completed at Deepdale Engineering in Dudley during the beginning of March 2015.

The new boiler is expected to be steamed during 2017 before being fitted to the frames.

The first outside cylinder was cast at the Coupe Foundry in Preston, on April 16, 2014, from a polystyrene pattern, manufactured by Premier Patterns of Smethwick.

The first tender acquired by the LMS-Patriot Project was formally handed over on May 4, 2010 and was completely dismantled that December. Sadly, the frames were found to be beyond economic repair as they were badly corroded.

An opportunity to acquire a second Fowler tender came in July 2012 when the East

Pete Waterman with supporters and officials of the new-build Patriot project at the launch of the boiler appeal at Crewe on May 19, 2012. ROBIN JONES

Lancashire Railway agreed to sell a spare one to the project. This tender had been acquired for spares for the Bury-based LMS 'Crab' No. 13065/42765, which was, at the time, being overhauled at Bury.

Also in ex-Barry scrapyard condition, this tender was found to be in better condition, with less corroded frame plates.

No. 4551 on display at the Great Dorset Steam Fair in 2014.
COLIN TYSON

BUILDING THE FIREBOX

The building of the inner copper firebox began in the LNWR Heritage workshops at Crewe in late 2013, after £130,000 was raised through the boiler loan scheme launched that October.

With the copper sheet for the firebox already obtained, thanks to a sizeable loan from a project member, and with the boiler drawings available, construction was started.

The smokebox, the first part of the boiler, had already been fitted to *The Unknown Warrior*. Now the heart of the boiler – the firebox – which is being made to the original design, began to take shape at the workshops, a short distance from Crewe Locomotive Works where the enlarged G9 ½in Claughton boilers were built, which were later fitted to the Patriot class locomotives from new.

Crowds of visitors to the Great Dorset Steam Fair over August 27-31, 2014, saw *The Unknown Warrior* exhibited as part of the 100th anniversary of the start of the First World War.

A display of special vehicles including tanks, traction engines, ambulances and even a petrol-driven Simplex narrow gauge locomotive, which would have seen action 100 years ago, were displayed in a special area of the steam fair, next to a re-created area of trenches that demonstrated the harsh conditions of trench warfare. Donations, sales, raffles and new memberships saw the project raise around £9000 during the fair.

A major milestone was passed, fittingly on November 11 – Armistice Day – that year. The fundraising reached the £1 million mark, a remarkable achievement in just six years since the project launch.

The Patriot firebox taking shape at LNWR Crewe on February 9, 2016. GAVIN SHELL/ LMS-PATRIOT PROJECT

The new Patriot takes centre stage at the Warley Model Railway Show. PAUL BICKERDYKE

AT THE NATIONAL MEMORIAL ARBORETUM

The National Memorial Arboretum is a site of remembrance at Alrewas near Lichfield, which honours the fallen, recognises military service and sacrifice and fosters pride in Britain.

A world-renowned centre for remembrance, it was officially opened on May 16, 2001. A registered charity, it is part of The Royal British Legion family of charities.

On November 21, 2013, *The Unknown Warrior* was taken there for a service of dedication, at which members of the Army, Navy and RAF were present. It was the locomotive's first public appearance away from its Llangollen construction base.

Two days earlier, over the November 9-10 Remembrance weekend, the partially completed locomotive was decorated with poppies in the Llangollen workshops.

After the ceremony in the arboretum, No. 45551 was taken for display at the 2013 Warley National Model Railway Exhibition, which had a Great War theme that year. Around 17,400 people attended the show at the National Exhibition Centre near Birmingham over the two days.

Once the show was over, *The Unknown Warrior* was taken to Tyseley Locomotive Works for the next phase of its construction to commence.

The Unknown Warrior on display at the National Memorial Arboretum for its service of dedication. LMS-PATRIOT PROJECT

The Unknown Warrior wears its poppies with pride in the Llangollen Railway workshops in November 2013.
LMS-PATRIOT PROJECT

A minute's silence was held at Tyseley Locomotive Works at 11am on November 11, 2015 to mark Remembrance Day and to remember all of the railway employees who lost their lives fighting in the Great War and subsequent conflicts. LMS PATRIOT PROJECT